Swiss Life:

30 Things I Wish I'd Known

Swiss Life:
30 Things I Wish I'd Known

Essays

Chantal Panozzo

Opyd Press
Chicago Zurich Somewhere In Between

Swiss Life:
30 Things I Wish I'd Known
by Chantal Panozzo

First published in 2014

Edited by Lizzie Harwood
Cover design by Igor Udushlivy
Book design by JD Smith

ISBN 978-0-9903155-0-6

Acknowledgment is made to the following, in which the stories in this collection first appeared, some differently titled or in different form: *The Christian Science Monitor*: "Your neighbor is not coming over to chat. She is coming over to clean your gutter"; *Brain, Child*: "The world's wonders are right in front of you"; *National Geographic Glimpse*: "Never underestimate the power of high-volume, Swiss German rap music," "How to speak Swiss"; *World Radio Switzerland*: "You can be fired in German"; *Expat Lit*: "Being foreign is fun 1.125 percent of the time"; *Hello Switzerland*: "There is nothing small about *Donaudampfschiffahrtsgesellschaftskapitän*"; *Count Your Blessings, Chicken Soup for the Soul*: "You can be fired in German"; *Multi-Tasking Mom's Survival Guide, Chicken Soup for the Soul*: "Guilt is universal"; *Swiss News*: "The Swiss know who you are better than you do," "'Flat' is Swiss for 'small mountain,'" "Switzerland may be neutral, but its laundry rooms are not," "You won't win an argument in German," "Switzerland is a freak show starring you," "The more German you learn the less you will talk," "Let your alphorn do the talking," "Nothing feels more foreign than a club filled with expats," "No matter how much you want a baby your wallet doesn't," "You can increase your cheese tolerance," "You are the scariest thing in Switzerland," "You will never be Swiss."

To my grandparents, who kept a 1970s menu
from a Zermatt café on a bookshelf in their
Chicago home for forty years.

Author's Note

Through no fault of their own, many people have come in contact with me during my years abroad. Most of these people were innocent. They had no idea the American they were interacting with was a writer of nonfiction. True, there were those who were aware of my writer status, but hung out with me anyway (were they crazy?). In either case, I would like to thank both the innocent and the not-so innocent by respecting their privacy. So that's why names have been changed and identifying characteristics have been altered. In addition, some timelines have been compressed or exaggerated in order to make the story read with a bit more interest than my fourth grade journal, which began each day of my life with the weather. If you'd like to read that version of my Swiss life, here's a start: Today it was foggy.

Disclaimer

Achtung, ladies and gentlemen.

Objects in this story may appear less perfect than you want them to.

Think of it this way: this book was almost called *A Bitch Abroad*. So if you're looking for a happy-go-lucky story about the glories of life in Switzerland, this isn't it. It's not a book about where to find the best chocolate, cheese, or ski slopes, even if the author has strong opinions on these topics along with a sweet tooth of consequence we will not get into here. And it's also not a book about the author's love for her adopted country despite the alphorn in her living room.

Instead, this book is about Swiss and expatriate life. The not-made-for-TV version.

It's sweet living in a place where the average person is thin despite eating twenty-six pounds of chocolate a year, but the experience shouldn't be sugarcoated. Because even if you live in a country as clean as Switzerland, life as an expatriate is messy. Trying to continue your life (rather than take a vacation from it) in a foreign place is a challenge as wonderful and daunting as the Swiss Alps.

I speak from experience. Eight years ago, I came to Switzerland to live the dream. Instead, I lived a life. Mine. Surprisingly it went on, and I did many more things during it than look for Heidi and eat fondue. I had an identity crisis. I found and lost jobs. And I became a mother. All while trying to learn one of Switzerland's official languages, only to find out most Swiss considered that a foreign language too.

Switzerland is efficient and idyllic, but my life living within its borders was not. So if you'd like to read a prettier version, I can recommend plenty of books and movies that will make living abroad seem like a beautiful dream. Or make Switzerland look like it belongs in a fairy tale rather than on a world map. In contrast, my version of living in Switzerland may make you cringe. Or feel uneasy. Or, hopefully, if you've ever lived abroad yourself, make you nod and smile. (But not smile and nod, which you've probably done enough of if you're an expatriate.)

So with that in mind, please sit back, relax, and enjoy some cheese and chocolate along with a good dose of sarcasm. And don't worry about that clock tower. It dings every fifteen minutes, 24-7. But you'll stop hearing it after awhile.

Contents

SWISS LIFE: 30 THINGS I WISH I'D KNOWN

The path from American life to Swiss life

1. Get fateful e-mail from husband: "I got the offer."

2. Google: "Should I move abroad?"

3. Eat lots of high fructose corn syrup.

4. Google: "Finding a job abroad. Hard?"

5. Toss. Turn. Repeat.

6. Wear sunglasses to cover up bags under eyes.

7. Remember who is president (2006).

8. Repeat #7. A lot.

9. Go to work. Stare at non-existent vacation balance. Shake head.

10. Realize looking back and thinking, "what if?" would suck.

What I Wish I'd Known
About Myself

#1: You will become a foreigner even to yourself

Two years after giving up my maiden name, I gave up something else: my American way of life. My husband's opportunity to work in Switzerland felt like a unique chance for adventure. So I agreed to go. I was Superwoman, after all. I believed I could move my house, my career, and our relationship as easily as the movers packed our dishware.

The dishes arrived at our Baden apartment, about fifteen miles west of Zurich, intact—they had been carefully padded. I, however, was another story. No one had bothered to bubble wrap my career, my marriage, or, most importantly—me. I don't know what I expected, but as a member of the Google Generation with everything from instant cappuccino to instant answers for "what is the capital of Vanuatu?" perhaps I assumed I'd also be graced with instant adjustment to the glamorous life promised by the term "expatriate." However, once the only thing I woke up for was to kiss goodbye a husband I barely recognized anymore (a suit? shiny shoes?), my new reality blared louder than the Swiss church bells: I had walked away from a fancy career at one of the US's top creative advertising agencies to go live as a housewife in a country most Americans confused with Sweden. At twenty-eight years old, Ms. 4.0-perfectionist-who-was-once-going-to-conquer-the-world-with-her-brilliance had instead become a passive follower: the trailing spouse.

In my early days abroad, I blamed Switzerland for my resulting identity crisis, but nothing was Switzerland's fault: its cows and geranium-filled medieval villages were there, just as promised. But the feeling of loss I experienced, which was about as deep as the ocean we had crossed during our move, became associated with my new country too.

Did I need a psychiatrist? Every book I had read about living abroad made me conclude that I should have been satisfied with eating cheese and chocolate and loving the landscapes. Instead, with every German lesson I completed, I became more and more frustrated by the incomprehensibility of my Swiss German world, which didn't sound anything like what I was learning in class. Hiding out in my Swiss apartment so I could live in a bubble and not talk to anyone, I read stories of American women living in Italy who described the Italian plumbers they couldn't understand as charming. I couldn't help but wonder, what was wrong with me? Why wasn't I finding misunderstandings amusing? People back home begged me to post all the fun I must be having on Facebook. How could I tell them that not being able to ask for an aspirin at the pharmacy gave me a headache? How could I tell them that despite Switzerland's well-marked 38,525-mile network of Alpine trails, I had managed to get lost?

What had I lost? Let's start with myself. Without the English language surrounding me, I lost my personality and I certainly wasn't about to post a status update on that. So I ran away to big cities like Paris, London, and Munich every weekend so I could brag about those instead. I was checking off things on my bucket list, but I was also running away from a place in Switzerland called "real life." Shockingly, it existed in small countries known for storybook mountain girls and I was scared to face it. Life was easier as a tourist.

Along with losing myself, I also lost the equality that had always sustained our marriage. Because even though my husband continued to treat me as an equal, after we moved for his job, there was a subtle shift in the balance of power in our marriage—and it was not in my favor. Brian had beat me to the boardroom while passing Swiss strangers reminded me that I was a failure at things as simple as putting my trash in the correct bags.

Being lectured by the general population on everything from a less-than-perfect garden to the way I recycled glass bottles (during the lunch hour, oops!) didn't make me a very nice spouse. Even though the Swiss tradition of social control had nothing to do with our relationship, Brian began to feel like a competitor instead of a partner. I couldn't figure out exactly why—maybe it was because we were the same age, had the same suburban Chicago background, or because we used to take the same quizzes side by side in economics class in college. He was my husband, but he was also my peer, and our relocation had altered the landscape of our relationship much in the same way a volcano changes an island's.

One evening, after my biggest accomplishment of the day had been to chase three birds out of our screenless apartment (but not before they had managed to poop on both armchairs), Brian came home grinning.

"I got accepted into an accelerated management program. They chose fifty people globally—the top 1 percent of the company," he said.

How did I feel about this? Oh, thanks for asking. Extremely pissed off.

Even though this was news that should have made me happy, it didn't. I had become a bitch abroad and it didn't make sense. After all, I had sacrificed a lot so Brian could work in Switzerland. I should have been thrilled with how well things were going for him. His win, my win, right? Wrong. Because I couldn't help but think that the top 1 percent—at least when we were in college—had been me. In moments like these, I admired my husband, but I resented him too. He had brought me to a place where foreign keyboards confused my "y's" and "z's." A place where I was no longer efficient or articulate. A place where I couldn't even read my mail.

I knew marriage was about compromise, but mail? I also never considered the one who'd be doing the most compromising would be me—that in one move, I could have lost so much of myself. What kind of modern woman had I become? I was not only a foreigner to the Swiss—I was a foreigner to myself.

As Brian stood there, grinning, I congratulated him on his most recent accomplishment. But behind my smile, a certain sorrow for myself simmered like a Bündner barley soup.

In German, there's a word called *Sehnsucht.* It doesn't have an English translation, but it described my feelings perfectly because it meant a kind of longing or yearning for what might have been. I knew we had moved to Europe to avoid thinking, "what if?" But while buying beef that turned out to be pork and watering my un-Swiss looking geraniums, I couldn't help but turn the "what if" into "what the heck has become of you?"

While Brian was in other places around the world becoming better prepared to manage all the thousands of IT professionals in it, I Googled for answers to my problems. Copywriting professor. Associate creative director. Writer for public broadcasting. I surfed the job postings from my graduate school's Facebook page, riding waves of little pixels, waves of hope for one last chance at finding the woman who had been lost. Résumés created, portfolios updated, there was only one problem: I had a husband with a great job nowhere close to any of my possibilities for defining myself in familiar ways. After about a month of looking out the window at the fog, I saw, for the first time, beyond it. If I was going to succeed in Switzerland, I couldn't apply for a job as an associate creative director in Richmond, Virginia. I had to create a new self, one that would agree with my new reality. And with that thought, a four-letter French word got stuck in my throat. Redefinition? It seemed like a challenge as difficult as pronouncing *Chuchichäschtli*, the Swiss German word for kitchen cabinet.

Not surprisingly, it was. Redefining myself abroad was the hardest thing I would ever do. Without a cultural grounding, my attempts at finding my place were as tentative as my German. But looking back, I can see that by finally accepting the idea of redefinition instead of denying it, the hardest part of my experience abroad was already behind me.

My husband helped. Most days, I received a hug and a "why don't you focus on your writing." Even though it took me an eternity to realize it (while the clock tower across the street reminded me exactly how long an eternity was), Brian was as much a "follower" of me as I had been of him. He came home for lunch when he knew I was lonely. He called from Beijing at midnight when he'd rather be sleeping. He asked his HR department to check my résumé before I submitted it to the Swiss world. With him at my side, I finally emerged from under the Alpine fog and into my new Swiss life. So what if I had followed him to discover it? Even though Switzerland had turned me into someone I didn't recognize for awhile, it also became a place where I ended up seeing both my country and myself more clearly.

How did I feel about that? Oh, thanks for asking. Extremely grateful for such a once-in-a-lifetime opportunity.

#2: The Swiss know who you are better than you do

Americans are obsessed with their heritage. "I'm 100 percent Polish, what are you?" they'll ask with a Chicago accent, some not even realizing where Poland is on a map. Like any good born- and raised-American, I also preferred to measure who I was in percentages: take one-quarter Italian and one-quarter Polish, and mix well with one-fifth English, 12.5 percent Danish, 10.5 percent Swedish, and 7 percent German. The result? Me.

I went to college in the heart of America's Midwest where I studied to be both an advertising copywriter and an opera singer. According to my American opera star professor, my 25 percent Italian heritage was all that mattered and my last name was to be flaunted. She worked with me to de-Americanize my offensive pronunciation of it and after my first year of study, I could say my name like an Italian native. When a fellow American heard me pronounce my newfound name they would say, "you're Italian, aren't you?" And I would answer with an enthusiastic, "yes."

So it was no wonder that after moving to Switzerland, I couldn't wait to discover my Italian roots. Just over the border, in the little town of Treschè Conca, Italy, I walked into a Panozzo furniture store like a typical American—as though I owned it. And even though it felt a little strange not to be able to communicate with the man in the store who was a supposed relative, for some reason, this didn't make me feel any less Italian. Instead, while I was there, I did the true American thing: I went shopping. I bought the cheapest piece of my heritage Mr. Panozzo had (a wooden coat hanger for ninety euros), took it home, put it in my closet, and called my trip a success. That piece of wood was an Italian piece of wood, chopped down directly from my family tree, and I proudly hung my Made-in-China coat on it.

My first name, Chantal, comes from the French, "to sing." But it had nothing to do with my heritage and everything to do with my American father's appreciation for high culture. Unfortunately, when combined with Panozzo, it announced to my fellow Americans that I was a foreigner in my own country. For years in America, I had cringed when hearing my name. I wanted to be Jennifer or Julie or Jessica not Shantel, Shartrell, or any of the other ways Americans pronounce French names. That's why it took twenty-eight years and a small country known for languages for me to finally accept my name. Because in Switzerland, with French and Italian as two of the four official languages, I finally, for the first time in my life, fit in. No Swiss person ever stumbled over my name. I didn't even have to go by "Liz" at Starbucks to avoid a ten-minute mix-up. To hear my name said correctly, and on the first try after twenty-eight years of mutilation, was a boost to my ego—never mind if the sentences that followed were lost in a German haze. At my first Swiss job as the lone English copywriter at a Zurich ad agency, I'd pore over the company phone list, admiring how my name actually felt like it belonged there. However, despite the way my name blended in, there was, unfortunately, the rest of me. My language options were English or English; I thought all cheese was bright orange, and I wore a baseball hat on the streets of Zurich.

Slowly and painfully, I learned to communicate in something other than English. Quickly, I learned that most cheese, even cheddar in its natural form, was actually white-ish. But for some reason, despite living in conservative, elegant Switzerland, I didn't do much to alter my casual clothing style. Zurich's main shopping street gleamed with Versace, Burberry, and Chanel. And I walked right down it in last year's Old Navy.

It took a few months, but one day I saw my reflection in the window of Burberry and actually compared it to what the mannequins were wearing. Then, I noticed that passing me on the street were skinny, stylish women sporting wool wraps, pencil skirts, and tall leather boots. They moved as if they weren't walking on cobblestones in heels—confident and fast. I tried not to notice that my Old Navy long-sleeved T-shirt had seen better days—like before it had ever been washed. And at that moment, it was obvious that my style needed to change. Because with one glance at my Nike-clad feet in a sea of stilettos, my true heritage had suddenly revealed itself. Forget my grand illusions of being a European hybrid, in fact, I was 100 percent American.

When you make a shocking discovery, you feel like you should do something about it. So I stepped into Globus, one of the larger department stores on Bahnhofstrasse. Like many Americans, I preferred large Swiss department stores to small boutiques because I was so used to shopping at stores the size of some Swiss cities, that a shop the size of a closet made me cringe. I preferred being watched by security cameras than actual people.

I took the escalator up to the women's department, where I fingered various exotic fabrics. Silk. Lace. Wool. As I tried on a lace wrap, I glanced at the price tag. Six hundred francs? I wanted to look European. But not that badly. I left the clothes on the rack in the dressing room and avoided the one roaming saleslady like she carried the plague.

Designer ambitions in the dust, I decided to check out H&M but the question was, which H&M? There were at least four of them on this street alone. I chose the biggest. Here, I found the prices more to my liking and the cotton and polyester clothes more to my style. I bought a black skirt and shawl figuring they'd look fine for my next trip to the grocery store, so long as I didn't wear or wash them before then.

So the next time I went out, I was dressed to impress. After dropping my baggy American clothes into the *Kleidersammlung* (clothes donation box), I dragged my orange IKEA cart filled with plastic bottles down the streets of Baden in bag lady fashion, but without my typical bag lady style.

In Switzerland, I had to redefine myself as a whole. Even with my new European fashions, I couldn't be 25 percent Italian. The Swiss didn't understand. They'd scratch their heads in confusion when I'd explain the pieces and parts of who I was.

"But you're from the States. You're American," they would say after hearing me spit out my statistics.

The next day, as I wandered through Zurich's old town in the first pair of Italian boots I had ever owned, I realized the Swiss were right about me. Even though I finally looked

European in my black skirt and uncomfortable shoes, in reality I was anything but. Embracing this conclusion, the next time I introduced myself, I pronounced my last name as I had originally learned it—the American way. Technically, it was completely wrong. But it never felt so right.

#3: Being foreign is fun 1.125 percent of the time

When I was young, one of my favorite books was *The Little Prince.* I especially liked the moment when the Little Prince realized he could be unique in the world despite the thousands of other little boys out there, if he learned to love someone.

I thought I could be exotic the easy way. Moving 5,000 miles from home to live in Switzerland surely had to make me different and interesting—at least to the locals. As an American, I was taught at a young age that I was unique, and I knew from watching television that I could become even more so by whitening my teeth and firming up my abs—in the United States, being extra special is only a few monthly installments away.

So I moved with high hopes of impressing the Swiss with my specialness, only to realize Switzerland doesn't reward individual uniqueness in the same way that American society does. I was tolerated to help the Swiss economy, but they didn't care about my extra white teeth or my shiny brown hair. Often, I didn't feel very well liked or even acknowledged despite my unique attempts at the German language—which involved speaking entirely in the present tense and trying to maintain at least a 33 percent score when it came to picking out correct articles. I wanted inclusion and recognition, but instead the Swiss people gave me distance and privacy—none of which I quite understood. Couldn't they see I was foreign and interesting? Didn't they like that I was witty and open?

Unlike the experience of my American mother, who lived in Gabon in the 1960s and told stories about all the locals touching her hair and admiring her "foreignness," most Swiss people can't tell I'm not Swiss until I open my mouth. And they certainly don't care one way or the other about touching my hair (not that I mind).

Three years after moving to Switzerland, I had almost given up the fantasy of being the exotic newcomer, until one day, while hanging out with some linguistically talented Swiss friends at the Sechseläuten Festival in Zurich, we noticed a couple of guys wearing *Lederhosen*. They were alone; so we invited these mountain men, clad in gold-plated cow suspenders, to join us in celebrating the Swiss tradition of watching a snowman being burned to oblivion to predict the summer weather, a twisted kind of Groundhog's Day.

The guys wearing Lederhosen were from Appenzell and had come to the "big city" to transport their horses to the festival. Unlike most of my Swiss friends (okay, my whole two Swiss friends), they didn't speak English or High German but that didn't matter. It was part of their allure since most Swiss like to correct not only my High German, but my English as well. These guys just kissed me (in the traditional Swiss way, on the cheeks, of course).

Through translation, my friends informed me that these men worked on a mountain in the middle of the Alps and did things like milk cows, make cheese, chop wood, and yodel.

The Appenzellers wanted to know where I was from, but "Chicago" got blank stares.

"Obama Town," I offered.

"She's from the town where Obama lived," translated my Swiss friend Hans.

Now I was a celebrity and I wasn't about to waste my fame.

"Can you yodel for me?" I asked, "All Americans—even those of us who have been here awhile—dream about hearing yodeling in Switzerland."

Before I knew it my request had been translated and the Appenzeller guys were giving me a private yodeling concert on the steps of the Zurich Opera House.

"It's no big deal, they learn to yodel when they're little," Hans whispered.

No big deal? I was thrilled. These two men represented the Switzerland that had been promised to me in the movies. Accordingly, I got out my camera to film them.

When they were finished, I asked if I could post a clip of their yodeling on YouTube. They didn't understand.

"She wants to put your singing on the Internet," translated Hans into dialect.

We don't have the Internet, was the reply. Wow, no Internet. These guys were growing more and more exotic by the minute.

"Please grill some sausages with us, American girl. We've never hung out with an American before," said the dark-haired one shyly.

I was their first? I had never been anyone's first American. But before I could figure out how to celebrate the one and only time I had ever felt appreciated for my nationality, my translators announced they were leaving and a funny thing happened. I wanted to leave too. The dream of being the beautiful foreigner had come true. And I wanted to preserve that rare moment in its purity—before I stumbled over communicating with the very people who found me so interesting.

"I'm sorry, but I have to go too," I lied. As the Appenzeller guys kissed me in parting, the blond one stroked my hair in the process. I couldn't wait to tell my mom.

#4: "Flat" is Swiss for "small mountain"

When people think of skiing in Switzerland, they usually imagine sleek skiers cascading effortlessly down the Alps. They are unlikely to picture an American expatriate sitting mid-trail in a mismatched snowsuit—five-year-olds swooping past her as if she were a tree in the path—while she addresses the pain in her tailbone and examines her wounded pride.

I didn't want to look like a foreigner on the slopes, so I tried to improve where I could. Sadly, I didn't consider skiing lessons. Instead, I figured a new ski suit would be the answer to my unfortunate skiing techniques. So after three years of pretending not to care about impersonating a ragamuffin, I finally looked professional, sporting a fancy, two-layered ski coat and matching accessories that didn't look like I grabbed them out of my mother's box of winter rejects.

The problem with looking good is that it makes your bad skiing look all the worse. It's easy to excuse a person wearing an oversized Land's End turquoise snow outfit from 1988. But put on a brand-new, black, white, and blue Spyder ski suit, and you're setting yourself up for complete and utter failure.

Because I grew up in the Chicago suburbs, I could make

lots of excuses for being a downhill skiing disaster. "Well, these people grew up on an incline," I would tell myself, as groups of Swiss retirees maneuvered skillfully past, while I tried to pretend I was actually in control of my thirty-one-year-old body when it was at a forty-five-degree angle.

"I am a child of the corn," I would repeat to myself as groups of Swiss four-year-olds waited for me to move after I was knocked down by the old T-bar—a plastic handle on the cable meant to bring me back up the bunny hill.

After four Swiss winters, though, I was fed up with being a downhill disaster. It was time to put all of that in the past and show the Swiss some of my real skills. My strategy: to do skiing the way I knew best—on flat land. After all, I grew up cross-country skiing in a suburban Chicago forest preserve. If anyone should be a master on a land of endless horizons, it should be I.

It had never occurred to me that Switzerland had any flat land, but once I inquired about this I was told otherwise. "Go to Einsiedeln," a Swiss colleague said, "It's flat there. It's where everybody cross-country skis."

So I went to Einsiedeln, a town about an hour outside of Zurich, ready to take on the Swiss. First, I went to the ski shop to rent some skis.

"Beginner," said the woman running the place, eyeing

my Spyder snowsuit, as she handed me what she deemed to be my proper set of cross-country skis. I wanted to protest, to tell her that unlike downhill skiing, I had been doing this cross-country thing since I was a kid. But my German didn't allow for such statements, so I figured I'd prove it to her by making myself a blur outside her window.

After five minutes on the course, I realized that the problem with cross-country skiing in Switzerland is that what the Swiss consider as flat land, I consider mountainous. So as a retiree lapped me for the second time on the six-mile loop, I slipped, slid, and panted my way up the Illinois-sized mountain—not even trying to keep up. "The way down will be easier," I told myself, but this wasn't true. I was at the top of a mountain in cross-country skis and there was something wrong about that. I paused, took a deep breath and tried to comfort myself in the fact that at least there was a pre-made track. But just because there was a trail for my skis did not mean my skis stayed in it.

As I crashed halfway down, the "Swiss Family Robinson" zoomed around me, leaving me buried under a pile of powder. As I sat there, cold, wet, and wondering how the heck to get up, I realized the only place I'd probably ever conquer as a skier was a forest preserve located 5,000 miles away in Warrenville, Illinois.

Like my German-language skills, no matter how hard I try, my skiing ability will probably never advance much beyond that of a Swiss toddler. But even though I don't like feeling like a two-year-old all the time, I'm sort of enjoying the part about being a kid. Especially when the sun shines on a stretch of actual flat land and I can pretend for a moment that I'm effortlessly racing through my own Alpine playground.

#5: You will be scared to go home again

On an expat contract, your life is like a reality television show with a really, really long commercial break. My commercial break was five years. So naturally, during it, I put off things for later, when I would return to my regularly scheduled American life again. My husband and I found ourselves saying things like, "we'll get a dog when we move back." Or, "we'll get a piano when we buy a house." Or, "we'll have a baby when we're living near family again." If. What. Where. When. These were the words that consumed our lives and I began to have a love-hate relationship with them. Instead of living my life, I was constantly putting it off: living a strange existence between reality and fantasy, as if I were somehow lost in space and time.

While it was often maddening to live a life on pause, I liked the bubble our expat contract provided. It came with things like international health insurance, free flights back to the United States, housing allowances, guarantees of returning home, and most importantly, the illusion that nothing would change—not even me.

But one day, I looked in the mirror and discovered some gray hairs. I was living a life put on pause in a medieval city center that seemed frozen in time. How could I have aged? As

I considered this, the clock tower across the street provided a badly needed wake up call: Ding. Dong. We interrupt this regularly scheduled expat contract to bring you a good dose of reality. The illusion of a return to normal is just that, an illusion. And by the way, your five years is up soon. Do you want to stay "permanently" in Switzerland or go back home?

Permanent was a scary word, so I took a trip home to see how home felt. The answer? Even scarier. I had been on US soil for approximately two minutes before I began criticizing Chicago's inefficient passport control lines and dirty luggage belts. Then, instead of running to the nearest place I could get a root beer with ice like I had done on previous visits, I criticized the sizes of beverages and the processed foods people ate with them. And I didn't stop there. I also criticized the unnaturally happy waitresses, the need to drive to get anywhere, the overweight people wearing pajamas in public, and the endless strip malls that were open 24-7. And then I even criticized myself for becoming a traitor because that's not who I wanted to be. I had gone from being a bitch abroad to a bitch at home. What had happened now?

Something called being an expatriate. While *Merriam-Webster* defines "expatriate" as "living in a foreign land," the dictionary fails to mention that after a few years abroad, an expatriate is more accurately described as "a person who lives somewhere between two foreign lands—one of those foreign lands being their home country." When I was in Switzerland, I felt foreign because I was foreign. But when I went home, I felt foreign too. It wasn't fair. As an expatriate, I was my own worst foreigner. I was changing and therefore challenging everything, whether I wanted to or not. A bitch at home, I'd find myself ranting about my own country in front of my family and stateside friends. "This is a country that cares more about sports than health care. This is a country that protects corporations instead of employees. And this is a country where the National Football League is tax-exempt but Americans living abroad are not." You name it, and I criticized it—right in front of the people I loved. I felt mean but I couldn't help it. I was seeing my own country through Swiss eyes now and it did not look pretty sitting in bumper-to-bumper traffic trying to drive to a place where I could take a run in the woods.

Not surprisingly, after this trip home, my husband and I chose to stay in Switzerland. No, we wouldn't have our expat contract and the bubble that came with it, not that it mattered since that bubble had burst during our last visit home. So my husband and I took out a new "permanent" contract on our Swiss life with all of the luxuries it provided—including a new illusion that we were becoming

Swiss. But about as regularly as a Swiss train schedule, I got into one of my American moods and railed against the lack of friendly strangers, the tiny portions with huge prices, and the absence of personal space. I wasn't homesick exactly, but something was definitely wrong with me.

My eventual self-diagnosis? Bubble loss. Life outside of my bubble was confusing and sometimes I wished I had it back. Because reality did bite. Especially when it made me eat a piece of Chicago-style pizza and realize it didn't taste like it used to. What the heck was I thinking when we moved abroad? I had been thinking adventure. Not of being ruined for life no matter what country I lived in.

Even though I had reached a point where I couldn't go home again, I would never fit in to my adopted home either. I was American, but I wasn't; I wasn't Swiss, but I was. Expats are possibly the most confused people on earth and I had permanently become one of them, floating somewhere between who I used to be and who I had become.

What I Wish I'd Known
About Neighbors

#6: Switzerland may be neutral, but its laundry rooms are not

In 1988, before I completely comprehended that the world was larger than my dead-end street in American suburbia, Switzerland moved in to educate me otherwise. Suddenly, living in a split-level ranch directly opposite my family's Naperville colonial was a woman who wore pants on hot summer days along with black socks and sandals. No matter that her fashion and accent said otherwise, her address confirmed her place in the neighborhood, so she became an involuntary subscriber to my monthly masterpiece, "The Fantastic Neighborhood News Magazine." No subscription necessary, this magazine was written and delivered by me, myself, and I, with a little help from my father who copied and stapled my masterpieces at his office. On lined notebook paper using red and blue Crayola markers and My Little Pony stickers, I published important events like fourth grade choir concerts, babysitting club meet-ups, and upcoming block parties.

I loved writing and I loved publishing and both came with nice job perks like neighborly praise. In fact, I had never met a neighbor who didn't seem to appreciate my little magazine and I secretly hoped the woman from Switzerland would take equal and approving notice of it.

Knock. Knock.

There she was, and she was holding a copy of my magazine. Thrilled to greet my newest reader, I rushed to the door. But Mrs. Schweizer didn't make small talk or thank me for the magazine. Instead she said, "You have a lot of mistakes in your writing."

Then, she did something no neighbor had ever done: she handed the magazine back to me. Inside, on the speckled Xeroxed paper, were corrections written in strange handwriting with a red pen. Misspellings, run-on sentences—you name it, and this non-native English speaker had found it. Her Swiss criticism was the American version of a slap in the face. Not used to being evaluated harshly by others, Americans have a saying, "you are your own worst critic." Not on our block, where needless to say, Mrs. Schweizer was not making friends.

Looking back, as neighbors, we should have had more empathy towards her; she hadn't been in our country long enough to understand that Americans are rewarded more for creativity and individual initiative than they are for punctuation and precision. And she also didn't know about the American "critique sandwich." This has nothing to do with lunch and everything to do with giving and digesting criticism gently. To tell a person what they did wrong, an

American begins and ends the discussion with what they did right.

Determined not to become the next Mrs. Schweizer, before I moved to Switzerland, I studied books on Swiss culture and traditions. I didn't want to make stupid cultural errors—I actually wanted to be liked by my neighbors. But even though the books I read taught me about Swiss efficiency and Swiss precision, I had no idea how they played out in real life except in places like the train station, where I knew to expect service exactly on time. It took becoming a foreigner myself to understand that culture cannot be learned; it must be experienced through trial and error.

Despite my attempted education, when I moved to Switzerland, cultural differences were most acute in the places I didn't expect to find them. Laundry rooms, for instance. How could a small chore like laundry become a big source of neighborly conflict? Yes, I'd have to revert to dorm-style living and share a washing machine in the basement, but my books hadn't prepared me for super high expectations concerning the proper removal of dryer lint.

My ignorance was American-sized and so was my load of laundry. Trying to cram it into a front-loading washer with the capacity of a large shoebox was impossible. As several shirts fell out, frustration set in. Even where to pour the detergent was confusing and the user manual, written in every language except the one I understood, didn't help. Finally, I shut the washer door and tried to regain the sense of control I had lost several weeks earlier by changing continents. Okay. Start the machine. 40 Sport? 40? 60 Sport? 60? 95? I pressed each button, hoping for a small miracle known as a wash cycle. Nothing. I was bewildered. I was dumb. And I had an audience.

"*Wiener schnitzel odor*," a voice said. I looked up. Why was this woman talking about dinner? Could she smell my helplessness? She was about five feet tall, but loomed large, peering down at me over a basket of towels. She had short gray hair, pressed slacks, and an annoyed expression. As embarrassment spread through my body like a case of poison ivy, my skin itched under her gaze. I didn't need an audience to share my stupidity with because that only made its encore practically guaranteed.

I glanced from this woman's leather shoes to her lipstick, silently wishing I could cover my head with the hood from my old client-freebie NASCAR sweatshirt. My toes gripped the soles of my flip-flops as though they were trying to hold on to some semblance of the old me, instead of this unwise woman who had slipped into them instead.

"*Function ear neat? Duh,*" she stood over me and flipped

a switch on the wall. The buttons on the machine blinked red, translating her speech into, "Duh, the machine wasn't even on."

She opened the soap dispenser and pointed at the middle of the three spaces, and then to the washing machine's user guide.

"*See moos lay sin*!" She shook her head, pointing to the German part of the guide, where every other word was about twenty letters long.

What should I say? I wasn't illiterate, but I was. I needed another official Swiss language and I needed it fast.

"*Deutsch, nein*," I said. "*Mais je parle francais. Un peu.*"

"*Bon.*" Looking relieved and not knowing that our definitions of "a little" were exactly one Atlantic Ocean apart, she flipped to the French section of the manual and pointed at some words. I shook my head, repeating "un peu." Then she shut the guide, gesturing like she was putting it into something. Putting the manual into something? Oh? Like the plastic bag I had thrown into the trash?

Besides the necessity to keep the instruction manual in a plastic bag at all times, the only other thing I learned that day was that everything I knew about laundry (and high school French) was worthless.

To her credit, this woman acted out elaborate

demonstrations to make up for my lack of sophistication in European languages and laundry customs. "Non," she said, turning off the dryer and shutting the dryer door. Then she opened the door halfway. "Oui." She repeated her actions, fanning me with the dryer door. "Non. Non. Oui. Oui." A bead of sweat ran down my arm. Not understanding much took a lot of concentration so I tried to relax and enjoy the breeze instead.

She extended her hand. "Frau Lanter," she said.

Was this her way of saying hello? I shook her hand. "Chantal," I said. I left out my life story due to a lack of a shared vocabulary.

"Chantal?" she repeated. I nodded, smiling because she had pronounced my name perfectly.

"*Mais vous n'êtes pas française*," she said.

I stopped smiling. It wasn't my fault I had a French name but wasn't French. I didn't know how to say, "It's a long story and it's my dad's fault." So I said, "*Je suis americaine*."

"*New York ou California*?" she asked. I shook my head. Did she think there was nothing else between these states?

Later, I discovered it was only fair that Frau Lanter knew nothing about America, other than what she saw in the movies. Despite my attempts otherwise, I knew nothing about Switzerland, except what I learned watching *The*

Sound of Music—and that movie was set in Austria. But I had assumed that any German-speaking country with mountains couldn't be much different from the next, just as Frau Lanter had probably assumed that America was nothing other than a celebrity-obsessed, mansion-filled country where people had huge kitchens but ate every meal from a fast food drive-thru. In our knowledge of each other's country at that point in time, Frau Lanter was the clear winner.

"I'm from Chicago," I said.

"*Shee-cah-goo.*" She nodded at me warily. And like that, the neighborly introductions were over, but the years of Swiss criticism were just beginning.

After the second installment of Nothing You Do In Switzerland Is Right, I began to look for Laundromats. I wanted a place where I could do my laundry as anonymously as the Swiss did their banking. Unfortunately, neutral locations to do laundry in a country that was supposed to be naturally that way did not exist, except in the format called washing machine ownership. Since my apartment had no hookups, I had to gather up my dirty clothes along with a good dose of pride, and persevere. In between major explosions for miniscule amounts of laundry lint (appropriate since our laundry room was formerly a bomb shelter), I began dreaming of the old days—twenty-one days ago—when lint barely registered as a noun, let alone something I should worry about. In Switzerland, no matter how hard I tried, I couldn't seem to clean the stuff out properly.

"Use this little paint brush," my neighbor instructed. "Really get inside the machine."

One particular day, after she had taken a pair of my pants out of the dryer (because the button was clanking around inside) and returned them after placing them in a small garment bag, I thought about the dirty laundry room in my apartment building in Richmond, Virginia. There, if someone's coins were singing a duet with their pants, you happily took the money out and used it to pay for your next load. If someone didn't clean out the lint, you didn't care. And people didn't worry themselves about turning electricity or water on and off. Exacting standards weren't our thing.

After eight months of Swiss laundry sessions, I was pretty sure there was nothing left for me to do wrong.

Except to think such a thing were possible.

Knock, knock.

Frau Lanter held a paper clip and imitated clanking sounds. She said something like, "I found this in the dryer. How careless of you."

I thanked her and took the paper clip.

Knock, knock.

Now she held the soap dispenser from the washing machine. You could remove it?

"Dirty," she said. "This must be washed." She handed me a bottle of vinegar and gestured what I could do with it. I tried to smile and nod.

Knock, knock.

This time, I hid in the bathroom. Just because I was doing laundry didn't have to mean I was home. But that was when I heard it.

"You're such a terrible neighbor," it said.

The little voice inside my head had spoken. I jumped up to grab a red pen, the perfect instrument to document how, for the first time since moving to Switzerland, I had been my own worst critic.

#7: Your neighbor is not coming over to chat. She is coming over to clean your gutter.

Don't get me wrong. I love planting flowers. It's just the watering, trimming, and weeding that I'm prone to forget. So naturally, I've always enjoyed the fall, when blankets of red and gold cover my neglected garden, causing me to forget for another few months that my thumb will never be green.

But then I moved from my tree-filled yard in Richmond, Virginia, to an apartment in Switzerland. While my new home included a wraparound balcony with an already built-in bounty of little bushes, herbs, and some other suitable plants, it did not include my usual cover, the tree.

Nevertheless, I was happy to inherit such a simple container garden. No grass meant no mowing, so with the extra time, I attempted some watering and trimming. And even though my Swiss geraniums failed to cascade in neat bunches over the edges of our concrete planters as Swiss geraniums always do, I considered myself a success and "planted" a little American flag in the midst of it all.

Of course, I couldn't compete on my neighbor's level. Over the summer, her balcony was filled with exactly 151 geraniums (all cascading in the proper Swiss fashion). Each plant was treated with the amount of care only she could give. Weeds were pulled out before someone like me could tell they were weeds. Fading flowers were clipped off before they had finished fading. And even in autumn, every stray leaf was immediately swept up.

While Frau Lanter called her container garden her "paradise," ours was about to be labeled a "*Katastrophe*."

Unfortunately, this was one of those German words so close to English that I could figure out its meaning. So there was no imagining she was praising my efforts when she appeared one week asking innocently, "May I go on your balcony?"

When I let her inside the apartment, she immediately ran out there, like an eager kid running from the car to a playground. It was then that I noticed she wore knee-high rubber boots and carried a trimmer, bucket, broom, and other foreboding items.

"This is a Katastrophe," she said, examining one plant after another. "These must be trimmed before winter." She looked in our gutter, dismayed at the mud and leaves that had dared to enter.

"This is a Katastrophe," she repeated, while I alternated between trying not to laugh and feeling totally ashamed. Then she looked behind each planter, where, unknown to me, rebel leaves were hanging out.

"This is terrible. These must be cleaned out. We are getting new windows next year."

As I tried to figure out the connection between new windows and stray leaves behind planters, my neighbor had gotten down on her hands and knees and was sweeping behind each one.

In between her sweeps and swoops, she glared at me, the hopeless non-gardener that I was, as if taking my lack of gardening ability personally.

I tried to make amends by sweeping as well, but everything I did, she made a point of redoing, so after a while I could only stare, my thoughts a combination of helplessness, amazement, and annoyance.

After sweeping, it was time for waterblasting the gutters, followed up with more sweeping. Two hours later, whether I liked it or not, my gutters were not just unmuddied, but unrivaled in their shininess.

The next day, she appeared at my door with a pressure washer. And I knew right away that balcony gardening boot camp, Part Two, was about to begin.

Even though a concrete balcony had never been on my radar as something to clean, there was no point in protesting. I was a foreigner in Switzerland, and it was time to learn from the locals.

So I let her in and six hours later, laid back and enjoyed my shiny concrete balcony complete with drinkable gutter water.

As I sank into my wicker chair, a weary boot camp survivor, I saw autumn's most recent victim—a stray leaf on my balcony. I thought it was pretty, but I knew that my neighbor would have been horrified. So in her honor, I scooped it up, gave it a lecture, and blew it off my hand, watching as it floated to the street below, where, fortunately, the street sweeper was just passing by.

#8: Never underestimate the power of high-volume, Swiss German rap music

My neighbor didn't only clean up gardens and lint filters, she also cleaned up people. Frau Lanter was a beautician, and somehow, this didn't surprise me. I imagined her tweezing eyebrows with the same gusto she reserved for pulling out weeds. But even after a year, that was all I knew about her—except that, according to her nameplate, her first name began with an "R." She always addressed me with the formal German *Sie* instead of the informal *du*, and I had yet to have a real conversation with her.

In some of my lonelier moments, I'd go through all the "R" names I knew–from Rose to Rhea–and wonder if I'd ever have an answer other than regret. I blamed my language skills for our lack of friendship, not realizing they were helping prevent me from telling a culturally inappropriate life story. Unlike most English speakers, Swiss people get to know each other over long periods of time, revealing themselves bit by bit. So in terms of developing a Swiss friendship, my small German vocabulary was *perfekt*.

About the time I was lamenting my failure as a neighbor, a huge party came to town: Badenfahrt, a ten-day festival filled with entertainment, parades, and fireworks. Music was blasted every night until 4 a.m., and the usual rules—like no recycling bottles after 8 p.m.—were completely abandoned. Instead, for ten days and nights I couldn't hear my phone ring. I couldn't talk to my husband without screaming. And I couldn't sleep. Our apartment faced the main entertainment stage; meaning I became educated in the secret reality that even Swiss-made concrete buildings can vibrate.

The ultimate Swiss party had come to me and I couldn't go home from it. So instead of embracing it and having fun, I became angry and confused because it was challenging every assumption I had ever had about Switzerland. The Swiss could be loud? The Swiss could be drunk? But there before me was the impossible, and he was pissing on my front steps. Beer bottles filled the square below my apartment and my shoes stuck to the pavement when I walked out my front door. The shiny garbage cans were overflowing like fountains while a gigantic statue of Lady Liberty celebrated the theme "World City Baden" in the Schlossbergplatz. Cigarette and marijuana smoke mixed with the smell of *Magenbrot* and sausages. The Swiss were partying harder in one short period of time than any Americans I had ever known. I scratched my head at the urgency of it all, not knowing that the answer to my bewilderment was right there in the Baden events calendar: Badenfahrt was a Swiss permission slip for scheduled madness. It was exactly what the Swiss needed to let loose: an organized reason.

Trying to escape the thumping bass one morning, I headed to the only quiet place around—the cold concrete floor of the laundry room. I was writing when Frau Lanter appeared. She was wearing a brown velour jogging suit—something much more casual than her usual pressed slacks and blouses. I blinked. Didn't the Swiss consider that kind of outfit sleepwear? Badenfahrt was changing everything—even my neighbor's wardrobe. Nevertheless, I braced for a laundry lecture, even if a little out of place lint seemed like an inappropriate discussion topic considering the chaos of my new and altered reality.

"Escaping the noise?" she asked. Her friendly tone matched her outfit. I nodded. My German had improved a lot in the last year and Frau Lanter now spoke to me in clear High German. "This is my fourth Badenfahrt! I've lived here for thirty-five years."

"And you...still here are," I said in my best German, amazed to be holding a two-sided conversation with her.

"I love Badenfahrt," she said. This also seemed to contradict everything I had known about her prim and properness up to now, but Badenfahrt was teaching me not to assume anything. Frau Lanter pointed to a charm on a thin rope she was wearing around her neck. "It's a Badenfahrt necklace. I collect them from each festival. Come, I'll show you more," she said, gesturing I follow her.

We took the stairs up to her apartment. As I entered, she turned around.

"Hi, I'm Regula," she said, shaking my hand like we had just met. Music from the street blared in the background, but it barely registered.

Was Badenfahrt transforming Frau Lanter into my friend?

"Come!" she said, grabbing a photo album and pulling me down beside her on a maroon loveseat. All around me, indoor houseplants—orchids, violets, and a delicate white flower I had never seen before—vibrated to the music.

Regula flipped through photos of past Badenfahrts—along with photos of all the cats she has ever owned: Schatzi sleeping in a laundry basket; Waldi swatting at a bird outside the window; Schnoerli hiding behind a geranium.

But where were all the people? Where were the friends and family members? I saw a photo of her niece who lived in France, but that was it. Regula had once told me she spent Christmases alone, and that was how she preferred it. But now, I began to wonder if that was true. Maybe she felt as lonely in Switzerland as I did sometimes.

The Swiss German rapper outside seemed to agree. "Ja,

ja, ja," he sang.

"Do you want some prosecco?" Regula asked, offering me a champagne glass. Had she addressed me with the informal "du" instead of the formal "Sie"?

"That's very nice of you," I said in return, using the formal version. She corrected me, insisting that I use "du." I repeated the sentence, informally.

Regula and I sat at the table and smiled at each other with a shyness that seemed out of place for two people who had shared a wall for a year. She tucked a few strands of hair behind her ear. Below us, the square was packed with people screaming along with the rapper; and the festival statues, including the gigantic Lady Liberty and a communist worker, lit up the background.

"Prost, Chantal!" Regula said, holding up her glass. Cheers.

"Prost, Regula!" I replied above the din.

Badenfahrt, I had decided, should happen more than once every ten years.

After I left her apartment that evening, I wondered if our newfound friendship would last. Because when the clock struck midnight on the tenth day of the festival, the street sweepers arrived by ding eleven and the city returned to its usual state of orderliness by ding twelve. There was no more thumping bass outside my apartment, Regula's geraniums were no longer askew, and bottles were no longer thrown into the street—or recycled after 8 p.m. If I hadn't known any better, I'd have thought the Swiss people were innocent. But there would always be one person who would remind me otherwise. Regula. She didn't go back to being Frau Lanter. In fact, she's coming over for dinner next week. I invited her, and she couldn't have accepted more quickly.

I guess that means I should go sweep my balcony.

#9: You won't win an argument in German

Regula stood outside my apartment in a pink rain jacket holding two pairs of shears. Before, this would have worried me, but a few years, a bit too much wine, and a German-English dictionary later, we had made peace. So much peace, in fact, that she was saying words such as "field," "flowers," and "drive."

Did she want to take me to one of those Swiss farms where you could pick flowers based on the honor system? Shopping without cashiers or security cameras certainly sounded exotic and interesting—if only I didn't have to get wet and muddy to do so.

I wanted to tell Regula that we should go flower picking another day since it was raining, foggy, and cold, but I (1) was not sure if a field of flowers was where she was taking me; and (2) realized that she already knew it was raining and foggy and that had never stopped her before. Rain never stops the Swiss because if it did, the Swiss would never do anything. Zurich gets even more rain than London.

What I also realized, as I followed Regula into the underground parking garage, was that she had purchased a new car and wanted to show it off. Not in the way that one would show off a bright red Porsche, mind you, but in the way that a seventy-six-year-old Swiss woman would show off a gray Opel.

"Fabulous gas mileage," I thought she was saying as she pointed to the dashboard, "and what a fantastic, adjustable driver's seat," she must have been saying, as she catapulted her five-foot frame behind the steering wheel.

We drove along and I tried to think of something to say. Well, I could think of lots of things to say—for example, how happy I was that she no longer lectured me about cleaning our communal washing machine's soap dispenser by soaking it in a bowl of vinegar—but I had to think of something that I could say in German. I'm not the world's best conversationalist anyway and a foreign language that uses verbs as afterthoughts kind of renders me mute. I didn't have to worry though, because we came upon a newspaper in the middle of the road and Regula had enough to say for both of us.

"Baden used to be a nice town, but now it's trashy, dangerous, and filled with foreigners," she said, as we swerved to avoid hitting the "trash" and almost sideswiped a Tex Mex restaurant.

I decided not to point out that we had now crossed the border into Wettingen and at the same time tried not to take the foreigner comment personally. Sometimes knowing a little German made living here more difficult.

The rain pounded on the roof of the car.

"Look," said Regula, showing me how fast her wipers could go.

"*Zuper*," I said, using one of those words that German and English have in common. Those words pleased me.

We drove into the green hills above Zurich and finally Regula pulled onto a gravel road and parked next to a field of cows. I didn't want to get out because it was wet and dismal and I didn't own a pair of gray "CHiPS" knee-high rubber boots like my neighbor (don't ask me where those came from), but I took the pair of shears Regula handed me and hoped for the best.

Cowbells clanged as I walked through the muddy field. I cut a few zinnias while Regula inspected the roses and called me over.

"Zuper," I said, looking at the wonderful peach rose she was pointing to. Everything in this field looked *schoen* to me and I wondered why the plants on my balcony couldn't behave more accordingly.

"Nein. *Nicht gut*," Regula said. And then she said something else and I didn't catch it at all so I shook my head.

"Sorry," I said, apologizing to what I believed to be a beautiful rose.

Satisfied that she had taught me something, Regula moved on to insult the daisies.

Meanwhile, I was drenched, I couldn't feel my toes, and the new Birkenstocks I had purchased at the grocery store to try to look more Swiss were now ruined so I threw some change into the farmer's bucket and ran for the car with my zinnias. I paused at the door because the car was brand new and I was dirty and I didn't know what to do. Our apartment's parking lot had a shinier floor than my apartment and if a newspaper on the road offended Regula I didn't know what she'd think of my mud-caked sandals.

As I stood there imagining what I could say to Regula: "Do you have a *Tasche* I could sit on? Should I put my shoes in the trunk?" she returned, empty-handed, and jumped in the car without taking off her boots.

"We'll try a different field," she said, looking at my pink and orange zinnias as though they were poisonous. "This one is terrible."

"Zuper," I said, wiggling my toes to see if they still had nerve endings.

Luckily the Opel's heat was as good as its windshield wipers. I tried to think of something to say (story of my life now), but then Regula put on the radio. "Radio Welle," she said, pointing at the station name as *yodelees* and *yodelas* filled the car. “Folk music, it’s beautiful. I play it when I clean too.” I nodded, picturing Regula scrubbing the moss off her balcony to the tune of “Bim Allenwindenturm.”

The next field was more to Regula’s liking and she took me to each flower, pointing out why it was worthy or not.

“Zuper,” I said, “Schoen.”

Regula pointed to another zinnia, but by the time we were halfway through the field at least 100 flowers had been insulted and only about ten had been picked.

I told Regula I was going to check out the gladiolas, and then I walked across the field, cutting what I found beautiful as I went.

Back in the car, she examined my pickings. She pointed at a flower in my bouquet, shook her head, and pointed at a flower in hers. I nodded as though she was saying, “My, what a stunning arrangement you have.” Because imagined dialogue or not, I was pleased to have developed such a real, honest friendship.

#10: Your apartment (and the rest of the world) is dirtier

Two minutes. That was how much time I had to watch a man, dressed in the official, city-of-Baden sanitation uniform, shine the public trashcan.

I was standing strategically on the train platform in order to (1) get a good view of the garbage can proceedings; (2) avoid breathing in too much second-hand smoke (I'm an American so I learned at a young age that the mere sight of a cigarette could kill me); and (3) keep an eye on the train departure sign so I could be ready to glare at the conductor should he arrive a second too late. I had a plane to catch so I wasn't in the mood to deal with the 1 percent possibility that this train could be tardy.

I had been living in Switzerland for four years so I was picking up certain habits: checking my watch to compare actual departure times to scheduled ones, talking quieter, smiling less, and asserting my body more. But some things still branded me as an American. And a fascination with Swiss cleanliness was one of them.

Since moving to Switzerland, I had redefined my definition of dirt. Things that I had never contemplated cleaning before were now on my radar. These included sink spouts, orchid leaves, washing machine soap dispensers, and concrete planters, although I wasn't necessarily doing anything other than acknowledging the fact that yes, even these items held the possibility of filth. Every once and awhile, Regula reminded me that my inaction was "nicht gut."

Earlier today was one of those times. I was over at Regula's apartment, giving her my mailbox key and telling her I was leaving for the airport in an hour, when, after showing me her orchids, whose leaves she had buffed with face oil, she mentioned she needed me to clean something. Urgently.

The gutter.

Of course. Everyone should have a shiny gutter complete with drinkable water and sadly, mine was muddied and Regula had probably been stewing about it ever since spring began. But the real problem, at least in my opinion, had nothing to do with my dirty gutter. The real problem was that I shared a gutter with a Swiss citizen and no American should ever be subjected to such hardship.

"Look at this dirt," Regula said, directing me to her balcony and pointing at the section where our shared, ground-level gutter became one and my foreignness revealed itself. Then she pointed at her fifty-one geraniums that were waiting patiently in a small plastic greenhouse.

"I want to plant them this weekend. But your part of the

gutter is dirty."

I sighed. Yes, I had neglected my gutter since the last time she had scoured it a year ago, but why did my half of the gutter affect her ability to plant her geraniums? I swallowed. The answer didn't matter. She was telling me to do something and my German was in a terrible place: good enough to no longer live in a "smile and nod" world, but not good enough to point out logic. So I muttered some words that wouldn't prompt me to have to talk any more than necessary:

"Okay, I will that make," I said in German, checking my watch.

Regula noticed the watch glance. The Swiss always notice things with time. But I was leaving in fifty-seven minutes and I wanted to take out the trash, close the windows, pack my toiletries, and print out hotel reservations, but alas, I was in Switzerland. So the dirty gutter would get priority.

"Just do the one section," Regula said, her version of being reasonable, gesturing over the big bush that separated our balconies.

"Okay," I said.

Back at my apartment, I walked past my half-packed luggage and went out to the balcony. On my hands and knees, I was trying to lift the six-foot-long metal grate off the gutter without causing any more back pain than necessary, when I saw Regula peeking over the bush.

"Be sure to get the leaves, too," Regula said. "Can I help?"

"Nein," I said, setting the metal grate down with a bang. I knew Regula would love nothing more than making my dirt a shared memory, but the last time she helped clean out my gutter, it took hours. I did not have hours. I had at most, five minutes, which for an American, was plenty of time to devote to a gutter.

I grabbed a small shovel and scooped out leaves and mud, hoping Regula would go away and play with her cat. Just because I spoke some German and expected trains to come on time, did not also mean that I had reformed my American cleaning style.

Regula said something, interrupting my thoughts.

"I will make it good," I said to Regula, realizing (dang!) that I had not used my verb as an afterthought.

Finally, a few scoops of dirt later, she was gone.

I breathed a sigh of relief, dropped the metal grate back over the gutter, printed out hotel reservations, welcomed Brian home from work, packed my toiletries, and then the clock tower across the street dinged once, warning us that the airport train would be departing in exactly fourteen minutes.

We rushed to the station, rolling our bags behind us. On

the platform, I admired the shining trashcan and the man who was cleaning it. The train departed right on time. And the man was still buffing as we pulled away.

When we arrived in Lisbon, I was about to admire the beautiful tiled buildings when I got distracted.

"Oh my God, there's a leaf on the sidewalk," I said. "And do you see the bird poop on that bench?"

Brian shook his head. No matter where in the world I went now, I always took a little Switzerland with me.

What I Wish I'd Known
About (Not) Talking

#11: Switzerland is a freak show starring you

Switzerland doesn't have much in common with Mars, but that didn't stop me from feeling like I had landed on another planet upon arrival. I smiled and the Swiss looked away. I said "*Guten Tag*" and the Swiss said "*Grüezi.*" I kept my personal space big and the Swiss invaded it like I was the globe and they were an American fast-food restaurant. Twenty-eight years after entering a world that I thought I understood, I had put on my usual white socks and sneakers and walked directly off an airplane and into a freak show where I was the freak. They call people living in a country without holding its citizenship "resident aliens" and it is not without reason. Back in 2006, I felt like E.T., big eyed and alone in an unfamiliar place, but with no way to phone home.

In the current world of smart phones and Wi-Fi, it seems almost impossible that connecting with my mom during my initial weeks abroad had felt like rocket science. But back then, no matter how I adjusted its antenna, my US cell phone wouldn't work on the European network nor would Switzerland allow me to sign up for phone and Internet service until I received my permit. And even though Swiss trains are efficient, Swiss bureaucracy is not. So my first month abroad was spent roaming the Swiss streets with my laptop, trying to find the Internet so I could communicate via Skype with family back home. Unfortunately in 2006, Wi-Fi was about as present in Baden as an out of place geranium. One of the only places the Internet was available back then was at the DuParc Hotel—but it cost SF 55 ($43) an hour to use it, which made Skype seem like a luxury good.

After a little Internet research that cost several hundred francs more than it should have, I learned that even permit-less, I would be allowed to purchase a pre-pay mobile phone since it didn't involve a contract. So I put on my big white sneakers and moved my little freak show to the nearest Swisscom store in the Baden train station. After determining that I could read nothing, which didn't take long since the entire store was about the size of one American parking space, I walked around conveying that I needed help. I picked up different accessories. I smudged sparkling-clean display cases. I paced from one side of the store to the other. Was fifteen minutes too long to wait for customer service or was it just me? Salesclerks orbited around me as though I were the sun. Accordingly, I started to sweat, burning up in a world without as much A/C as my old one.

As I shifted from one foot to the other, I finally came to the conclusion that when you're observing a new place, you cannot just stand there and stare at it. You've got to listen to what it is trying to tell you. Once I did this, I was able to hear that the salespeople were speaking into microphones every few minutes, calling out something that possibly resembled numbers. Why they needed microphones in a store of this size I didn't try to figure out because I was concentrating on finding the Take-a-Number dispenser, which I had walked right past on my way into the store. Grabbing a number, I held it tightly and said it to myself in German. I stood there waiting, muttering, as people came and went. Sixty-five. *Fünfundsechzig.* Fünfundsechzig. Fünfundsechzig. After another fifteen minutes passed, I realized the clerks must have called my number without me understanding it.

Embarrassed, I turned as red as the Swiss flag. That I was having so much difficulty doing simple things in Switzerland surprised me. China or Kenya, sure, maybe I would have accepted a few challenges there. But Switzerland wasn't supposed to be a land of hardship; it was supposed to be a land of cheese, chocolate, and tax evaders. Things were supposed to be easy and delicious here. Instead, I couldn't even understand numbers I had studied or get service in a store.

What could I do? I wanted to give up, but I had once read that people who live abroad are more creative than people who do not. It would be nice to prove this theory correct, even if my current reason had more to do with desperation than with inspiration. So I thought for a moment, and then went back to the number dispenser and waited until a young woman entered the store and took a number. Then I took the next number. Now I wouldn't have to listen for numbers that for some reason did not resemble numbers in any of Switzerland's official languages. I relaxed—slightly—satisfied that forty-five minutes after entering the store, I might actually be deemed worthy of Swiss customer service.

After the next few numbers were called, the young woman with the number right before mine, on whom I'd been depending for all future communication, turned to me and said, "Do you speak French or English? Because I can't understand a word they're saying."

"I can't either," I replied. She gave me a look of defeat and I echoed it. With no patience left for anything—including creativity—I crumpled up my number and threw it like a meteoroid high above the shiny surface of the Swisscom store and watched with satisfaction as gravity had its way with it.

#12: The more German you learn the less you will talk

After the Swiss authorities finally deemed I was worthy of purchasing a cell phone and installing a landline, a strange thing happened—Swiss German speakers began calling. So there I'd be, casually picking up a call, thinking it was going to be my husband or mother only to realize it was Frau Zo-and-Zo from who-knows-where telling me something so foreign and threatening that I even lost the ability to ask if she spoke English.

My first phone call in German was so traumatizing that I started hanging up on any caller who dared to speak it. Later, after I had been educated in both Swiss phone etiquette and the German language, things got more complicated because there were more options to consider. Gone were the days when I could start a call with a casual American "hello" and end it with a "good-bye." Now I had to consider the Swiss version of answering the phone, which consisted of barking "Frau Panozzo" in a monotone that wasn't me. Sensibly, I decided I would challenge established Swiss phone norms and use American phone manners, only translated.

This meant that when my phone rang in Switzerland, I would say "Grüezi" and then wait for a response. Usually, my grüeziing resulted in silence on the other end while the Swiss caller got over their initial greeting shock and tried to figure out how to talk to a confused person like me. But instead of going with the flow and saying a "grüezi" back, after their pregnant pause, which I had to admit I fathered, my Swiss caller would revert to their own style of phone conversing, stating a name like "Frau Moser" which naturally made me reply, "Nein, ich bin Frau Panozzo." And then there'd be even more confusion because they hadn't been asking my name, they had been sharing theirs.

So my hellos were hell and then there were my good-byes, which hadn't been good since moving to Switzerland. The cardinal sin of Swiss phone etiquette is to forget a caller's name by the end of the call, so even though I'm not religious, I found myself praying every time the phone rang. The main problem was that while I was trying to remember a caller's name so I could say "Auf Wiederhöre, Frau Moser," at the end of the call, my mind would also be working so hard to process the topic of conversation, that the name of the caller would get lost along with everything else. When the caller would bid me "Auf Wiederhöre, Frau Panozzo," I could only say a pathetic and plain "Auf Wiederhöre" back. I would then hang up in shame, a woman with a master's degree in communications having failed once again at saying good-bye.

In the process of learning language skills and cultural curiosities, I lost any sense of how to talk. On the phone, I couldn't read lips, facial expressions, or emotions. I couldn't mime, pick up props, or make elaborate gestures. On a phone, all I had were words that flew at me faster than I could catch them. And while a lot of Swiss people speak English, these were not the people who dialed my number so I began to regret both my desire to own a phone and its invention. Sometimes I pretended my phone didn't exist.

"Your phone is ringing!" Edi would say, a Swiss colleague who had the unfortunate fate of sharing an office with me in Zurich.

"Phone? What phone?" I'd reply, pretending to be deaf.

I learned to set the ringer as low as possible and only answer calls from Brian. Anyone else was forced to leave a voice mail since then I had the option to repeat the message, not that I had much intention of calling anyone back.

Phone fear turned into e-mail addiction. Over time, I learned to conduct any and every foreign communication possible through e-mail since it put two things on my side that a phone didn't—time and Google Translate.

Finally, two years after moving to Switzerland, if a caller spoke in German, I might actually understand a few phrases. And since I was tired of feeling stupid, I began to pretend I wasn't. So after barking my name, I'd say "ja" and "*genau*" when appropriate and then I would say good-bye, usually not having a clue about the overall point of the conversation.

One day the secretary called, saying Herr Schmidt was here to see me. I panicked, wondering if he was the same guy who rang yesterday wanting to show his hexyskajf and have a biengkdalge. After pacing my office, I grabbed a business card and went down to greet him, trying to act like I was in control and knew exactly who he was and what he was doing here.

"Hallo, Herr Schmidt," I said in my best Deutsch, shaking his hand.

"Hallo, Frau Panozzo," he said, "Based on our talk yesterday, I brought my aiemdng so we can wokdnanb about the ieknbdg."

My cell phone rang. I didn't know who it was, but this time, I didn't care.

"I'm sorry," I said pointing to my phone, "but I have this call to take."

"No problem," said Herr Schmidt, taking a seat while the secretary asked him if he'd like his water with or without gas.

I ran out of the room and back to my office, telling Edi that I had an important call and he should go down and deal with Herr Schmidt. After Edi left, I was about to answer my phone when the call went to voice mail.

I leaned back in my chair and put my feet on my desk. Maybe my Swiss phone was a fabulous thing after all.

#13: There is nothing small about *Donaudampfschiffahrtsgesellschaftskapitän*

"What can I bring you?" Many a thoughtful guest asked this question before coming to visit. Suitcases poised and open, they expected answers like Jif peanut butter, Kraft macaroni and cheese, or Oreo cookies. How could I tell them I wanted the greeter at Wal-Mart? The co-worker who said, "How was your vacation?" The cashier who asked me if I was having a party since I was buying so much beer? I wanted the one thing my guests couldn't pack: a pointless exchange.

"So how many inches will it be today?" Mandy asked.

It was my first trip home after living in Switzerland for six months. But I wasn't just in a hair salon in suburban Chicago. I was also in heaven. I was wearing a black cape and being pumped skywards in a black pleather chair, and all I could see in the mirror was my big white smile as I said, "I'm thinking five inches!"

Five inches. A unit I could comprehend in a language that was mine. I giggled more than is naturally acceptable over the word as Mandy massaged my head with shampoo. As she combed and cut, we talked.

"You got plans for the weekend?"

"Spending time with family!"

"That's always nice."

"How about you!"

"Oh the usual: friend's party, bar hopping."

"Wow! Sounds great!"

Brown ringlets fell to the ground, little half moons decorating the white tiles as we talked about nothing. Nothing. The conversation was wonderful. I considered asking for another inch off so I could stay longer. With conversation that good, I could have gone bald.

In Switzerland, I often found myself longing for this kind of exchange. Because when people talked in my German-speaking world, there was nothing small about it. Each word was at least fifteen letters long and none of them combined to ask me about my weekend. In Switzerland, people thought small talk was superficial and false. If there was nothing important to say, they preferred silence.

Without small talk, I was awkward. Naked. My Americanisms shined in all their glory when I began a meeting with, "So I hear you're going to Geneva today?" instead of, "Here are the ads we created for your product."

Saying hello and then immediately presenting work made me cringe even after three years of doing it. I would have been much more comfortable, if I could have at least found out what everyone had eaten for lunch before launching into business.

During meetings between Herr Thisandthat and Frau Panozzo (oh yeah, me), I found myself getting nostalgic for my client meetings back in the States. Discussing a client's dog's bout of fleas, I'd think, those were the days. Now I couldn't even use first names, never mind anything else that might have had an element of personality.

Office walls speak volumes about the kind of conversations that go on within them. The more personal the items on the wall are, the higher the level of personal exchange. In my Zurich office, the only things on the walls were charts and ads. However, in my former office in Virginia, the walls weren't walls—they were shrines. You knew whose kids played soccer, who had a cat, and who had gotten married, without even asking.

In Switzerland, small talk didn't only fail to exist in offices, but also in everyday life. Even Regula didn't waste any time with, "Boy, it's hot out," before launching into her usual tirade about how Baden used to be a nice town, but now it was dangerous, trashy, and filled with foreigners. Maybe she would have gotten through to me better if she had commented about the constant fog before ranting about the foreigners—but the weather didn't appear to be part of the German vocabulary.

For me, the lack of small talk created a big emptiness.

It took being 5,000 miles from home for me to realize that inane interactions were an important part of my life. I could prepare myself for the other things—like stuffing my suitcase full of Rice-A-Roni to beat cravings for processed food—but some things, like small talk, couldn't cross borders.

Thank goodness I could. After stepping off the plane, I gave my family a hug.

"Hello, how are you?" I asked in my best small talk. Then I rushed out the door in search of a meaningless conversation with a cashier to discuss with rare enthusiasm the possibility of getting 10 percent off by opening a store-sponsored credit card. And then, I skipped to that pleather throne, surrounded by the queens of small talk who masqueraded as beauty professionals. In this little, suburban, Chicago salon—more than anywhere else—small talk was larger than life.

#14: Let your alphorn do the talking

Did you know that besides throwing out your garbage incorrectly there is one other way to connect with the normally reticent Swiss?

Neither did I. And strangely enough, this secret conversational method has nothing to do with putting your trash on the corner an hour too early and everything to do with the proximity of your body to an alphorn. Whether the ten-foot instrument is slung over your shoulder in a backpack or you are attempting a tune in the town square, the alphorn inspires a conversation as easily as Swiss National Day inspires a farmer to serve breakfast to 500 strangers.

The credit for the discovery of this secret Swiss social networking tool goes to my husband. I was traveling to Paris for a writing workshop and he was worried he'd be bored in my absence. He decided nothing would solve his boredom like alphorn camp. So there, on the top of the appropriately named *Hornberg* ("Horn" mountain) near Gstaad, my American husband learned to play the alphorn along with sixteen Swiss musicians.

I dismissed Brian's alphorn extravaganza as a passing fad, but a month after his intensive weekend course, a rental alphorn made its way from Davos to our living room. The first time he practiced the instrument, whose sound can travel for eighteen miles, I wondered what Regula (who only practices her electronic keyboard with headphones on) would think. I didn't have to wait long to know. Shortly after Brian's first notes rang out, our doorbell rang too. Before I could apologize for the noise, Regula had run into our living room and applauded my husband's performance.

Later we realized that once you become an alphorn player in Switzerland, the absence of its sound could start a conversation too. Because when Brian didn't practice for a few days, Regula would come over to ask me why. "It's important that he keep playing," she would tell me. "The alphorn is good for integration."

Regula was right. Not that we hadn't tried to integrate in our pre-alphorn days. We just weren't very successful, despite our attempts at learning German and smiling at the locals. We learned the hard way that in most Swiss situations, you don't need to tell people why you're buying so many sausages; you just need to stop talking so much and exist for a while (or for many years) before you will be accepted. The time it took for us to make friends in Switzerland wasn't personal; it was cultural. For Regula, it took a year before she told us her first name. For office colleagues, it took a few months before we could share a coffee. But here's a secret for English speakers looking for instant involvement: none of the Swiss waiting and formality applies if you carry an alphorn.

The alphorn is the great Swiss-foreigner leveler. Who would have guessed? Certainly not me. I hadn't realized the power of it until my husband took it with us on a trip to Bettmeralp, a resort town near the Aletsch Glacier. Like usual, we packed practically for a trip requiring four train transfers: bringing suitcases, tennis rackets, a bag of food, and also a ten-foot horn. To our surprise, however, the alphorn lifted us out of foreign awkwardness and into the rare world of Swiss acceptance. We had been on the first train for approximately two seconds when a man sitting across from us leaned over like an old chum and asked, "Is that an alphorn?"

One transfer later, the train conductor told us about his alphorn group and two transfers later, a woman asked which were our favorite alphorn songs—then went on to tell us her husband had composed some of them. The fact that Brian and I would answer these questions in German—but with bad grammar and an American accent—only made the Swiss talk to us more. They wanted to know where we were from, where we lived, and how long Brian had been playing the horn. Each encounter proved that the Swiss—who are normally very private—would quickly embrace a foreigner, as long as we demonstrated a visible interest in their culture. Luckily for us, nothing is much more visible (and audible) than a ten-foot horn.

During our evenings in Bettmeralp, Brian practiced his alphorn. I was only too happy to hear it in a space larger than our living room, and would sit on a blanket near his chosen location and observe how the music echoed across the mountains. The first night, he drew an audience of about fifty cows, who are naturally drawn to the alphorn's soothing tones. But on most of the nights that followed, the Swiss did too. As I lay on my blanket listening the following evening, a mother and her two little boys came out of their chalet and walked across the field towards us. The boys sat quietly with their mother, applauding at the end of my husband's practice session before begging for an autograph.

After my husband bid farewell to his newest fan club, we walked across the field to a restaurant where we were greeted by a smiling waitress (yes, smiling) who wanted to know if it was "he" who had been playing the alphorn. Then, two minutes later, along with our beers, she also brought out the chef, who was able to cook up not only some alpine macaroni, but also a few stories of his alphorn touring days.

Unfortunately, the alphorn is not particularly easy to

carry. Nor is it easy on my ears in the apartment. But I have accepted this. Because while the Swiss may not comprehend my American smile or my attempts at High German, my husband's alphorn they understand. So even though the German language is very hard to learn in a Swiss German-speaking world—especially since small talk fails to exist—the alphorn makes it a little easier. After all, I can only learn to understand the Swiss if the Swiss are willing to have a conversation.

#15: How to speak Swiss

At first, the train announcement was in French. An hour later, it was in German. Then I got off the train and everyone was speaking Italian. Being the one-language wonder that I was, I took an Advil and reminded myself that I was in Switzerland, where people often use multiple languages in the same sentence, where crossing the Alps is like crossing the border into another country, and where somehow everyone manages to understand one another—everyone, that is, except *moi*.

As a proud holder of a GA Travel Card (Swiss train pass), I crisscrossed the country counting not only how many peaks above 13,000 feet I could see exactly on schedule, but also how many confusing linguistic situations I could be put in within a space the size of an American basement. One of twenty-six cantonal pieces at a time, however, I began to solve Switzerland's linguistic puzzle and develop my own little guide for how to speak "Swiss."

French (Western Switzerland)

To the uninitiated, western Switzerland is more like a region of France than a region of Switzerland. The Swiss French enjoy their wine and have large festivals celebrating the grape harvest. They fill their streets with brasseries and outdoor cafés. Any French-speaking Swiss will make it clear that they are *not* French. But be prepared to speak French. In this region, English is at best a consolation prize, and German? well, the Swiss French prefer not to admit they have anything to do with such a language.

At a bar in the Romandie (With a soccer game playing on the television)

Bonjour, parlez-vous allemand?
Hello, do you speak German?

Oui, mais vous ne voulez pas?
Yes, but you don't want to?

(The bar explodes with cheers for the German soccer team, who has just scored a goal against France.)

Dans ce cas, pourquoi encouragez-vous l'équipe allemande de football?
Then why are you cheering for the German soccer team?

Parce qu'ils ne sont pas la France? Je ne suis pas sûre de bien comprendre.
Because they aren't France? I'm not sure I understand.

Italian (Southeastern Switzerland)

The southern side of the Alps feels like a different world. In fact, should you find yourself in southeast Switzerland, you might wonder if you have accidentally crossed the border into Italy. There is sunshine. There are palm trees. Every other shop is selling ice cream. And the buildings are all painted yellows, oranges, and pinks. Plus, every restaurant serves only two things: pizza and pasta. Suddenly disoriented, you might find yourself needing directions:

Asking Directions in Italian

Mi scusi, come arrivo al lago di Como?
Excuse me, where is Lake Como?

Attraversare la frontiera? Veramente pensavo di essere già in Italia.
Across the border in Italy? But I thought I was in Italy.

Oh, *sono ancora in Svizzera?*
Oh, I'm still in Switzerland?

Adesso capisco perchè non si vede smog.
Ah, that explains the lack of grime.

Ma, e le palme?
But what about these palm trees?

E com'è che la gente parla italiano?
And why are people speaking Italian?

Ah, *e così, gli svizzeri parlano anche italiano.*
Oh yeah, Swiss people speak Italian too. Figures.

German (Most of Switzerland)

Even though German is the most commonly spoken language in Switzerland, you probably won't recognize it. Because it's not the German you learned in school—and it's not the German the Swiss learn in school either. Swiss German is an unwritten dialect with variants that change approximately every mile. Versions of Swiss German can be so different, that even Swiss German speakers don't always understand each other. This suits them fine since they appreciate secrecy. But for foreigners who don't, here's how you know you're in a German-speaking area: The street sweeper is on constant duty, the shopkeeper is more concerned with wiping down the counter than serving the next person, and small talk doesn't exist.

Speaking German to a Cashier at the Grocery Store

Grüezi.
Hello.

Ich mache eine Party. Deshalb kaufe ich so viele Chips.
I'm having a party. That's why I'm buying a lot of chips.

Aber aus irgendeinem Grund gibt es in diesem Laden kein Bier.
But for some reason there's no beer in this grocery store.

Oder Cheddar. Das ist doch das Land der Käse, oder?
Or cheddar. Isn't this the land of cheese?

Sagen Sie nichts?
Aren't you going to say something?

Irgendwas?
Anything?

Ja! Ich habe eine Cumulus-Karte! Dank der Nachfrage!
Yes! I have a store loyalty card! Thanks for asking!

Romansh (Mountainous Region of *Kanton Graubünden*)

Romansh is spoken by roughly 60,000 people—less than 1 percent of the population — who are scattered in tiny, rural towns throughout Kanton Graubünden, in eastern Switzerland. Romansh doesn't appear on food labels or Swiss job search sites. Yet it is an official language of Switzerland, so it appears on formal Swiss documents. But since more and more young people are leaving Kanton Graubünden, and the forested, mountainous region is sparsely populated to begin with, it's starting to feel a bit empty.

Speaking Romansh to a Cow

Hallo? Ei cheu enzatgi?
Hello? Anyone?

Nua ein tuts auters?
Where the heck is everyone?

Hallo vacca. Ti eis la suletta, che jeu anfla per tschintschar.
Hello, cow. You're the only one I can find to talk to.

Mi plai tiu sgalin. Astgel jeu far ina fotografia da tei?
I like your bell. Can I take your picture?

Di "cheese" = caschiel!
Say cheese!

Wow. Bien Echo.
Wow. Cool echo.

Gesture

Given the frequency of communication breakdowns in Switzerland (at least for foreigners), it's also common to communicate through good, old-fashioned body language. Here are a few acts or gestures you could try, no matter what part of the country you're in:

Kissing the air around someone's cheeks three times.
Hello.

Setting a huge bag on the bus seat next to you.
Sorry, this seat is saved.

Standing inside the entrance of a restaurant for a really long time.
Hi, I'm an American and I have no idea I'm supposed to seat myself.

However you attempt to communicate, remember, in Switzerland, language confusion is nothing out of the ordinary—23 percent of us are foreigners, after all. In the world of linguistics, the Swiss are the champions. The rest of us enjoy the breathtaking landscapes with a side of speechlessness.

What I Wish I'd Known
About (Not) Working

#16: Nothing feels more foreign than a club filled with expats

Not long after giving up my career and moving to Switzerland so my husband could advance his, I signed up for the international, adult version of "rush week": in other words, I registered for an orientation program at an expat women's club.

I had never been a "sorority, organized-social-event, buy-my-friends" type of gal, but the program supposedly helped you settle in and meet other English speakers. To justify my participation in something so prearranged and purposeful, I told myself that I was only going to attend the orientation. I wouldn't actually join the sisterhood, even if there didn't appear to be any Greek letters involved.

The problem was, once I arrived at the clubhouse, I heard a lot of English and I liked that. I hadn't been surrounded by so many English speakers in what felt like decades—even though it had only been a few months since my arrival in Switzerland. The thrill continued when Nikki, the woman in charge, spelled my name wrong on my nametag.

"Welcome, Shantel," Nikki said, handing me the nametag. I smiled at her pronunciation of my name. Nothing said I was home more than hearing my name butchered.

As I went to find a seat, stopping at certain points to

eavesdrop, I realized how much I had always relied on institutions like school and work—not to mention the English language—to make friends. I had never considered how lonely life could be if, suddenly, you had none of these things to rely on. Maybe I had been wrong. Maybe a club of expat women was exactly what I needed.

"Welcome to our orientation program for newcomers to Switzerland. I'm the club president," Nikki said.

Everyone clapped, so I clapped too. While we were giving her an encore, Nikki sipped something tall from Starbucks and I stared at her outfit. She was wearing a red Chanel suit (one that made sure that everybody knew it) and coordinating red lipstick. Queen of the expats, I thought.

I turned my attention to her royal subjects; the English-speaking ladies sitting around me, who were all new to Zurich even though most of us had gone out of our way to disguise our foreignness. No white gym shoes. No sweat suits. No pajamas in public. Just form-fitting dress clothes that would make you think we were all employed by multinationals. Maybe that was the point. I looked down at my newly purchased leather flats. I barely recognized myself.

"Before we begin, let's introduce ourselves—where you're from; what your husband does; what company he works for, and how many children you have," Nikki said.

I sat up straighter and looked around, waiting for the protests, but there were none. What our husbands do? How many kids we have? As Nikki made her introduction to serve as the shining example for all of ours, my mouth hung open in disbelief that such patriarchy still existed and that women knowingly supported it.

Nikki came to Zurich via Paris, London, and Cape Town, and her husband was the CFO of Some Big Bank; she had three lovely children aged nineteen, twenty-one, and twenty-three, each now living on different continents. The next woman wasn't much different, except her name was Jenni and she was from: "that's a hard question, so let's say Toronto"; her husband was the COO of the Same Big Bank, so surely he knew Nikki's husband. It was a small world and she had 2.5 kids that went to Zurich International School.

One by one, wives of lawyers, executives, and bankers introduced themselves—their identities served by their husband's position—each blending into the next: an endless wave of dutiful nomads, questioning only where they called home.

Finally, a twenty-six-year-old woman introduced herself as Samantha. She made a point of stressing that she was an actress who used to perform shows in the West End. She wanted to give singing lessons while she hung out with her

Swiss lawyer boyfriend, who she had met while waiting tables in London. Samantha gave me hope.

Then it was my turn. "Hi, my name is Chantal. I'm a copywriter from Chicago and I moved here from Richmond."

Samantha turned around and winked at me as I sat down, awaiting another woman to emerge from the wives. But as I sat there, finding none, I remembered: in Switzerland, we were "*Frauen*": a German word that makes no distinction between "woman" and "wife." So, I sat back and sulked.

Later in the program, we learned about crime in Switzerland (not much to learn), how to recycle paper (much more complicated than crime), and how many of the sixty women present actually put their kids in a free Swiss school, as opposed to a 30,000-francs-a-year international school (one woman). But the thing I learned that day that affected me most was this: I had felt like a foreigner in the very group of women where I was supposed to have felt at home. In that room, on that day, I was the strange one. The one in my twenties who was new to the whole trailing spouse world and therefore not at peace with my place in it or with those who had accepted their fates. So even though finding an advertising job as an English copywriter in Switzerland seemed almost impossible, it surely had to be easier than finding inner peace with my trailing spouse identity. And it would also prove that I wasn't a passive follower; I was an assertive career woman.

That night, my job search began.

#17: You can be hired in English

I was sitting in a white room, at a white table, in a white chair, and staring at a white cabinet. I was wearing a black tank top, black pants, and uncomfortable, pointy-toed black shoes and reveling in the fact that Roman, the white-haired secretary (dressed in a white linen pant suit), was bringing me a bottle of Pellegrino and a glass.

Elegant. Europeans would never drink directly from a bottle, so I resisted my animal-like American urges and poured the bubbly water into the little glass, remembering how I used to drink tap water out of big Styrofoam cups at my last job.

The CCO of IDEA was late. I didn't think Swiss people were ever late because if I invited Regula over, she stood outside my door until the clock tower across the street dinged in coordination with our agreed meeting time. Ding, dong. Knock, knock.

As I waited for my impending interview, the lack of A/C, the shiny white table, and the white walls started to make me dizzy. But then Herr Müllerbach arrived, shook my hand, downed an espresso, and said, "Chantal. Thank God you're here!"

I smiled at the sound of my name being said correctly

and on the first try. I was not in Kansas any more (or at a particular expat club, for that matter).

As Herr M examined my portfolio, I held my breath, hoping my American résumé and way of presenting my work were okay. Copywriting interviews were always awkward because where were you supposed to look while your interviewer went through your portfolio? At the top of their head? Out a window? At your work? This interview was no different, except for the desperation that radiated from me like heat from the sun. I wanted to continue my career. I wanted to do things other than laundry and to meet people who defined themselves by more than what their husbands did. I pressed my hands together to keep from fidgeting.

Herr M shut my portfolio.

"We need you. We need an English copywriter. We've been looking for months. There are none in Zurich," he said, drumming the table. "Except you."

He stood up and paced the room, his fingers running through his hair. All I could think was, they need me. I am wanted. I have found a place I can belong in Switzerland.

But then he said, "We need you to write direct mail."

Direct mail? My heart sank like the *Titanic*. I was used to writing national television commercials and print campaigns for glossy magazines. Direct mail was not for me.

Direct mail was for losers. Everybody in advertising knew that.

"The client wants the work done in English first and then they'll translate your writing into German, French, Italian, and Romansh."

Okay, well maybe direct mail in five languages was sort of sexy. But actually, it didn't matter. I was a desperate foreigner in Switzerland who would do anything that involved a feeling of acceptance. Even (insert small, despairing sigh—) write direct mail.

"Why don't you meet the creative director?"

Two minutes later, a man came in; a tall, elegant, Swiss creative director, wearing black-rimmed glasses, a tailored pink button-down, black jeans, and shiny black leather shoes. Had he been in a movie?

"Schmidt, Hans-Paytah. Hallo." He shook my hand.

"Hello Mr. Schmidt," I said, looking at his outfit while admiring that unlike most of the creative directors I had known in the US, he actually ironed and didn't appear to choose his wardrobe from his high-school-aged kid's closet.

"Call me Hans. Hans-Paytah." Was that spelled P-a-y-t-a-h? Or was it Peter? As in Heidi and Peter?

Hans-Paytah opened a window. Then he lit a cigarette. I pretended not to notice and tried to breathe normally. If people smoked in the office, how had the walls stayed so white?

Herr M handed Hans-Paytah my portfolio and drummed the table. Hans-Paytah leaned on the windowsill, smoking. He laughed at my Miller beer campaign (it was supposed to be funny) and flipped through everything else like it didn't matter.

He and Herr M spoke to each other in German for a couple of moments while I tried to maintain my feeling that I had found a place I'd belong. As they were talking, Herr M's cell phone rang. He answered it in French and talked for a few moments, his fingers running through his hair. Then he hung up, "au revoir," said something to Hans-Paytah auf Deutsch, and turned to me in English and said, "Hans-Paytah thinks you can also work on other projects at the Zurich agency, he can translate your stuff, yes?"

"Okay."

"What do you think, you have the job."

He pushed a bunch of papers across the table. My eyes widened. It was a work contract. They had prepared it before they had even met me. I guess I hadn't been the only party who was desperate here.

As I calculated how underpaid and overworked I had been in the United States, I hid a grin by taking a sip of my

Pellegrino. Madison Avenue had nothing on, uh, whatever Swiss *Strasse* I was on.

"Can you start next week?" Hans-Paytah asked. He said something to Herr M in German.

"Sure. I mean, ja." The sooner I could experience a sense of belonging in Switzerland the better.

"Zuper," Hans-Paytah said.

They both shook my hand.

"*Danke.* Auf Wiedersehen," I said.

On my way back to the train station, I glanced in my bag every few minutes to make sure the contract was real and it was still in there. I didn't want to lose my new lease on Swiss life—even if I had sold my soul to a world of multilingual junk mail. Because this wonderful and strange world of Swiss advertising promised to be a place where I would no longer be an awkward outsider, but an insider—a real member of Swiss society with a business card and a +41 phone number to prove it.

#18: Schmooze in German at your own risk

At some point in most abusive work environments, it occurs to one party that their earnestness is being used against them like a weapon, that their efforts are paying for someone else's champagne, and that they should get out before they become more frustrated than a fly stuck in a spider web. I'm sorry to tell you that this didn't happen to me. Instead, despite an absent boss, a group of employees I could barely understand, and a non-native English-speaking client who thought my English did not sound native, I still displayed the hope of a Girl Scout peddling thin mints to an office where people preferred nicotine. So I wore my American work ethic with pride, smiling and nodding as most of the agency's multilingual workload landed on my desk and their second-hand smoke funneled into my lungs.

It was almost impossible to think that there could be a smokier environment than the IDEA office. But there was. It was called a Swiss bar before 2010. When Rolf, the big boss of the IDEA network, came to Zurich, the meetings for our creative department were held at a bar in Niederdorf, an area of the old town. As usual, today's meeting began with Rolf blowing smoke in my face. I could hardly breathe, but I leaned in to give myself the best shot at comprehension. It was hard enough to understand German in the office—even with my weekly classes—but at a bar, it was even worse; in addition to music, clinking glassware, and laughter, there were also my two creative colleagues, Edi and Anja, who each spoke in their own Swiss dialect.

"I fired Hans-Peter," Rolf said, putting out his cigarette and lighting another one immediately. "That's why I called this meeting."

"Isn't it great?" Anja said, flipping her long hair over her shoulder. She touched Rolf's blazer, while crossing and uncrossing her legs, her skintight jeans tucked into her stiletto boots. She pulled out a pack of cigarettes from her leather jacket and continued to say something I couldn't comprehend. Even though she knew I was learning High German, Anja spoke only in Swiss dialect when I was around.

Edi, Rolf, and Anja all started talking at once, Rolf in German and Edi and Anja in Swiss dialect. I wouldn't have been able to understand this concoction if we had been in a soundproof studio, but I feigned fluency anyway by smiling, nodding, and trying to coordinate my reactions to match theirs. I checked my watch. I'd been there for only five minutes but it felt like five hours. I was in for a long night; trying to pretend I followed a conversation was ten times more exhausting than actually understanding it.

I gulped my prosecco and ordered another. The more I drank the better my German got. I had to do something to stop feeling stupid and start fitting in.

Edi, my only office friend, filled me in a few times with English translations:

"It was because of the prostitutes."

"And the porn."

I had never been so sorry to not understand Swiss German. I made a mental note to study more.

Then Edi told some kind of joke and Anja and Rolf laughed. I laughed too. My laugh was high pitched and calculated. It wasn't my real laugh. But I was safe; they wouldn't know.

The leather couch was sticking to me. I could feel a bead of sweat about to run down my skirt and into my black knee-high Swiss boots. Anja's pack of cigarettes read: "Smoking endangers health." As I considered holding my breath, Anja lit another and blew the smoke in my face. I blinked, my eyes watering, but noticed that her pack was now empty, and I enjoyed this small victory. I excused myself and went to the bathroom. I'd never considered going to a bathroom to enjoy the fresh air, but compared to the bar, the bathroom smelled great. After admiring the impossibly clean toilet, I fanned myself with paper towels and then blotted my forehead.

When I returned, Anja was buying another pack of cigarettes from the bar's vending machine. My stomach sank. So much for my little victory.

"I was just telling Rolf about the pink tuxedo that I got in LA!" Edi said. I smiled, pleased to hear my language for a minute, but then Anja sat down and English once again lost its world domination.

Edi started telling another story, his arms gesturing like he was Italian.

I laughed and nodded, even though I hadn't a clue what he was saying.

"You understand Swiss German?" Anja asked.

"Some," I lied. The others weren't laughing anymore. Maybe Edi was saying that his brother was in an accident. My face reddened and I turned away. Outside, everyone walking by was wearing black coats, making the streets of Zurich resemble a giant funeral procession despite the backdrop of the brightly colored houses of the old town. But maybe it was my mood. American rock music dominated the German conversations around me and its familiarly only emphasized my loneliness because like the music, I didn't quite fit in. I swallowed and checked my watch (9:05. Only?). Then I turned back to the German conversation before I did something drastic. Like leave.

Then Rolf, Edi, and Anja put on their coats and I could hardly believe my luck until Rolf said,

"Next stop, Haifisch!"

Anja giggled. I didn't see the humor in yet another smoky bar, but at least we were now outside. The fresh air greeted me like a long-lost friend. I breathed in deeply and coughed, choking on the fog. Before I moved to Switzerland, I didn't know you could do such a thing. Edi and I followed Anja and Rolf to the next place. Anja's heels clicked on the cobblestones. Edi got a call on his cell, so I had nothing better to do than to will Anja's ankle to break. But somehow, each little heel found the exact middle of a cobblestone as she walked.

Rolf waited for me by the door of Haifisch.

"I can't wait to see your expression," he laughed.

Outside was a glowing neon fish logo. Inside was a stage with poles. A young, blonde woman dressed in a black teddy and fishnet stockings was singing. There was one pregnant-looking man ogling her from a little silver cocktail table. My mouth was also hanging open.

It was refreshingly not smoky since there was no one here on a Tuesday night, but Rolf and Anja soon took care of that.

I read the menu. The glasses of champagne were the

equivalent of $65 each. Rolf ordered four, despite recent gossip that the agency wasn't doing well.

"Two extra vacation days if you go up on that stage and sing, Edi," he said.

Then opportunity arose because Teddy Girl had finished her song and was now sitting at our table between Rolf and Anja, like she'd known us forever.

They lit up again and she basked in their smoke, introducing herself as "Natalia."

I wasn't usually grateful for half-naked women at my table, but upon her arrival, the night immediately improved because Natalia only spoke English (and Russian). So I gave her a smile. A half one.

Rolf called the waiter, "A glass of champagne for the lovely lady," he said, leering down her lacy top. She tugged it lower for his benefit.

We learned that Natalia had been working here for a year but didn't strip; she just sang in skimpy clothes.

"Well, we're looking for a secretary," Rolf said, handing her a business card, "and you'd be perfect."

She admired the card and stuck it in her underwear.

In the meantime, Edi was discussing the possibility of singing on stage. "I've got a new pink tuxedo. It's from LA. But I didn't bring it with me tonight," Edi was saying to the waiter, and I could tell Edi regretted this since he usually did have a spare tuxedo with him at the office. But no matter. Two minutes later he was onstage, basking in the spotlight, wearing jeans and a Ralph Lauren button-down. But from the look on his face, he was in black tie regalia.

As he sang, a woman appeared from backstage and started pole dancing while Edi crooned. The disco ball in the center of the room turned, creating little stars across the stage, and Edi tried to catch them. During the interlude, Edi set the mike onto the stand and joined the stripper on the pole, who was now wearing nothing but a thong. As Edi and the stripper rubbed against each other, Anja laughed, and I automatically mimicked her.

Anja leaned over.

"Now this is what real people in advertising do," she said.

"Genau," I said. *Exactly*. But I wasn't sure whether I should laugh or cry at the truth of her statement.

Edi, sweaty but beaming, high fived us all after his song. "Two extra vacation days!" he sang. Then he took off his glasses and wiped his face with a napkin.

"For a job well done," Rolf added, his arms now around both Natalia and Anja. Natalia clapped.

Edi was flushed, pleased with himself. He beamed. If I hadn't known any better, I'd have thought he had given an

#19: You can be fired in German

In Switzerland, it's possible to get hired in one language and fired in another. I should know, because it happened to me. As my recently appointed German- (and German only) speaking boss shut his office door, gesturing that I sit on his couch and pulling his chair closer than any American-sized personal space concept would ever allow, I knew what was coming. After my three-year stint as the Zurich advertising agency's only native English-speaking copywriter, I was about to become the next victim in a long line of worldwide economic tragedies.

I was losing my job. And the only word I could say was: danke.

"Danke?" my boss laughed, after he told me the advertising agency decided to let me go because of money problems—and language issues. In a way, it was a relief. Because the combination of my bad German and his bad English made our communications a series of linguistic nightmares that only seemed bearable due to my constant smile-and-nod technique.

For the last four months, I'd attempted to communicate with my new boss using all the tools that my two-plus years of German lessons would allow. I spoke in short sentences, limiting myself to either past or present, and made sure that every possible *der*, *die*, *das*, *den*, *dem*, *denen* or *des* was properly disguised as a "duh."

But it was no use. Working as an English copywriter in a German-speaking environment wasn't going to work without someone like my first boss: a linguistically talented Swiss creative director who could take one look at my English copy and ideas, and automatically understand almost everything—except sometimes the sarcasm.

As I sat through my new, but soon to be former boss' layoff speech, his German passed through me in two categories—what I understood, and what I didn't. I heard I did things well—but in the wrong language. I heard that he would try to help me find another job—but with people who understood English better than he. And I heard he would write me a *Zeugnis*—whatever the heck that was. And then he hugged me, something—after watching too many episodes of *The Apprentice* with a sneering Donald Trump yelling, "You're fired!" before shoving his victim out the door—I didn't know a firing involved.

The next part was even stranger. I had to go back to my desk.

Staring at my layoff letter, which I had to sign in order to be officially let go, I read the German paragraphs. May

31, said the letter. My last day at the agency. I looked out the window at the snow. It was February 26. And I wasn't sure how I should act from now on, let alone find the motivation to create ideas. Luckily Edi was out to lunch. So I had at least an hour to figure it out.

Three months to work. Three months until unemployment. Three months to pretend everything was normal. Trying to continue like nothing out of the ordinary had happened after being laid off was a new experience for me. In the United States, I had witnessed people getting kicked out of the office the moment they were fired. Frantic, these former colleagues would ask those of us with jobs to save their files before their computers and last few years of their lives were snatched away. Sometimes they'd sneak in at night to print a résumé or some portfolio pieces to help them get their next job. And here I was, back at my desk, with full access to a color printer and company e-mail, trying to figure out how the heck I could possibly write another witty headline at a time like this.

The reality was, I couldn't. Bank copy didn't flow, but personal questions did. Why had I said "danke," to my boss? Was I thankful? Actually, yes. I wasn't grateful to lose my job, but I was thankful for being allowed more than three months to collect my work, print my CVs, and look for a job—all while being employed. After all, it is not in an American's upbringing to think being laid off means anything other than a sneering boss shoving you, ashamed and humiliated, immediately out the door.

So after lunch, I tried to hide my numbness and continue working like nothing had happened.

"Chantal is the best," my boss said, after I confirmed that I would be fixing the copy on the bank ad.

Right, I thought. *That's why you laid me off.*

That night, my phone rang at home. It was Edi.

"I heard they had to let you go," he said. "But guess what? I quit!"

This was the best news I had heard all day. Edi had found a new job, so he had given the required three-months notice. This meant we could spend the next three months becoming more and more unmotivated together.

The following week, Edi's status was announced at the weekly company meeting but mine wasn't. Nevertheless, when people came into our office, they gave Edi looks of admiration while I received looks of pity—if people even acknowledged me at all. The whispers had started and they made me contemplate hanging a sign above my desk saying: "I was fired. So now you know."

"I'm sorry to hear you're leaving," one of the designers

said to me, like it had been my decision.

"Danke," I replied.

No matter how hard I tried to make work seem normal now, it wasn't. So I started to lose my original gratitude for having three months to work. All of a sudden, it seemed that at least if I had been kicked out the door American-style, I would have been past my sorry state by now and on to better things. But instead, I was whispered about, ignored, and had every job-searching move criticized by my boss, HR, and most of my department. Being laid off Swiss-style meant I wasn't a job seeker. I was a job loser. And having to go to work with that label meant I couldn't do the thing I wanted to do most—move on.

My apathy for the whole situation started to show. I wasn't in the mood to create ideas. I wasn't in the mood to attend meetings with people who no longer made an effort to speak High German with me since I was far from comprehending the mystery of Swiss German. And I wasn't in the mood to handle the little things either—like the woman who always criticized my lunch.

"So much garbage," she'd say, pointing a finger at my prepackaged salad.

I stopped eating in the lunchroom even though I felt like a grade-school loser. I either ate at my desk or went out to lunch with Edi so we could countdown our final weeks together. Not surprisingly, our lunch breaks got longer and longer as the three months wore on. One day, we went to the zoo. Another day, we snuck out at exactly at 5 p.m. (which is like leaving before lunch in advertising time) and went to his house to watch a movie. While Edi strategically put his umbrella and bag near the front door so no one would see him leaving early, I couldn't have cared less at that point and walked out in front of everyone in full rain regalia.

As if on cue, my boss looked up.

"What are you doing?" he asked.

"I'm going to watch a movie," I replied.

"No, I mean after working here. What happened on your last interview?" he asked.

"None of your business," I wanted to say. Except my German skills didn't allow me that luxury. So I said nothing.

"Well I've got a headhunter and I told her about you," he said.

And what did you tell her? I wanted to ask, that you laid me off?

"Give her a call, she has jobs for you," he said.

I wasn't desperate enough to take job advice from the person who made me redundant in the first place, so I mumbled my word of the month: "danke." And then I walked out.

Calling my boss's headhunter aside, I debated a lot of things at work during this time. Like whether I should give my boss a cool idea or let him suffer.

I gave him the cool idea.

"Wow," he said. "You're good. This is a great idea."

"Yes, don't leave us," said the intern.

I wanted to scream. But instead I smiled and shook my head.

As my projects dwindled from few to none, I didn't have much to do besides a bunch of paperwork from HR, so I turned my attention to compiling CVs and job search material. I prepared a 20-page document and then debated printing it out.

"Well, what's the worse they can do, fire me? Wait, they already did that," I thought.

So I clicked 'print.'

As the weeks went by, I printed personal stuff more and more, and my boss talked to me less and less. One week, he said a total nine words to me: "Hello. Do you have any cookies? No cookies. Oh."

Maybe he was mad that I didn't call his headhunter.

By mid-April, I had no projects and no one (except Edi) talked to me—other than behind my back. So I did what anyone in this situation would do. I went home and cried. Worse than losing my job was the fact that I was losing my confidence. When June came, I'd be the trailing spouse all over again, someone with nowhere to go—while her husband traveled the world—but into depression.

One day, to boost my self-esteem, I opened Lotus Notes and reread e-mails from the good old days when I was a valued member of the organization. As I was enjoying the message announcing an award I had won, my boss actually came in to acknowledge my existence.

"It's stupid for you to be sitting around," he said. (I mean, after all, I wasn't even listed on his "who's doing what" chart in the hallway anymore.) "You have no work to do. I'm going to tell HR we should let you go a month early."

Wow. The company might actually release me of my contractual obligations? I couldn't wait. Pleased to be possibly looking at freedom from my fired status, I said what I always said to my boss these days—"danke."

But this time, I really meant it.

#20: You can reinvent yourself again

As most unemployed people have probably done, I made a conscious effort to disguise my status. I styled my hair. I pressed my slacks. And I smiled a lot. If anyone was ready for the "Information Day for the Unemployed" it was I. But instead of finding myself among other manicured go-getters, my fake American extroversion and optimism made me stand out like a bald eagle in a world of unassuming Swiss swans. Contrary to everything I had assumed about human nature and unemployment, I discovered that the redundant Swiss didn't spend a lot of time trying to pretend they were something other than jobless. Instead, they sported jeans and blank expressions. Some of them appeared as if they had been out of work for years as opposed to a week, and I couldn't understand it. Were these the same people who dressed up to go to the grocery store? Who wore leather dress shoes on the hiking trails? Who would never be caught dead wearing pajamas in the communal laundry room (except during Badenfahrt)?

As I pondered this, the person walking into the seminar room behind me said, "*Grüezi mitenand.*"

"Grüezi," everyone mumbled back, obediently.

Then another person walked in.

"Grüezi mitenand," he said. "Grüezi," the room murmured.

Great. Not only had I worn the wrong clothes and the wrong expression, but I also hadn't followed Swiss custom and greeted everyone when I walked into the room. I squirmed in my seat, took out my notebook, and doodled.

At exactly nine, a woman with short blonde hair marched in, said, "Hello everyone," and slammed the window shut while we all grunted a "hello" back.

She introduced herself in Swiss German and I groaned inwardly, ready for my brain to tire out after its two-minute tolerance for the local dialect. But then I heard something pleasing:

"Would anyone prefer I speak in High German?"

I swallowed, waiting for someone else to admit their foreignness first.

When this didn't happen, I raised my hand, trying to disappear at the same time I made myself known. All eyes turned to me; I had just identified myself as the foreigner in the room and my face turned a Swiss geranium shade of red. I shrugged as if to say, "Sorry, I live here."

Frau Speaker switched to a clear High German, which was rendered clearer by her slides and handouts, which summarized everything she said. I sighed as relief flooded my body. For once, I had been rewarded for admitting I didn't fit in.

*

Later that day, inside the elevator of my apartment building, I faced the mirror.

Who had I become?

I turned to examine myself from the side and adjusted my posture.

Glamorous expat? No.

Trailing spouse? Well…

Unemployed foreigner?

I ran out of the elevator and into my apartment before I could answer that question.

*

A few hours later, my phone rang.

"Hello," I said, answering American style. I had a headache. I couldn't deal with any more Deutsch today. And if anyone tried one of Switzerland's other official languages, well…

"Chantal, this is Dave, the director of World Radio

Switzerland," a deep voice said, in English.

My heart skipped a beat and I gripped the phone. I had applied for a freelance job with them a few weeks ago during my days as "the fired girl."

"We're interested in your idea about discussing unemployment in Switzerland."

"Oh. That's great."

"But what about making it personal? You're a writer. So how about writing and performing a four-part series about your story?"

"That sounds interesting."

"I think Swiss people need to understand what it means to have to keep going to the office after you've been laid off. So what do you think?"

I couldn't think. I was too excited.

I hung up and called Brian to brag about my new job.

An hour later, however, I was biting my nails. The assignment from World Radio Switzerland meant I would have to admit to a few thousand listeners that I was an unemployed loser. A little voice in my head told me this was not such a good idea. Confused, I stood in front of my bookshelf. I scanned the titles, my eyes fixing on David Sedaris' *Holidays on Ice*. This had been his radio debut—writing about how demoralizing it was to be an elf at

Macy's. I scanned the other memoirs I loved—*Running with Scissors*, which revealed the insecurity of being gay and *The Glass Castle*, which discussed a childhood spent in poverty. All the books had one thing in common: bad experiences that made good stories. If I were going to reinvent myself as a writer, I'd have to rub nail polish remover on my desire to present myself as the glamorous expat and international businesswoman I had never become. I needed to let my shame shine. I knew who I was: an unemployed foreigner who was going to be proud of it. I sat at my computer and stared at a blank Word document. It stared back.

To procrastinate, I checked my inbox. You could say the alumni newsletter came at the wrong time. As I scanned through the successes of former classmates who hadn't tried to work in a country where they didn't speak the language, my breathing quickened and I felt nauseous. What had I done with my life? Then Brian walked in.

"What's wrong?"

"You. Don't. Understand."

"What?"

"I. Got. The. Alumni. Newsletter."

"So?"

"It's. Not. Fair. Karen. Is. A. VP. Now."

"Well, whatever. You're a VIP of the Swiss government."

"Yeah. That'll. Look. Good. On. The. Résumé."

"Just enjoy your freedom for awhile."

I pointed at a pile of German unemployment paperwork.

"Freedom. Sucks."

"Well, what about your radio gig?"

"Yeah."

"What do you mean? I thought you were excited about it."

"That's before it sank in that I'd have to admit to thousands of people that I'm unemployed."

"Who cares?"

"I do."

"Come on, admit to failure for once. And if you do it well, you'll be a success."

"Right."

"Don't give up the opportunity. Come on, let's have dinner."

Brian's BlackBerry beeped and he silenced it. I wished I could switch off my mind too.

*

A lot of people have issues. They need to stop smoking. They need to come out of the closet. Or they need to get sober. But what I needed to do was to get over myself. This shouldn't have been so hard. The reason the radio station wanted me to share my unemployment story in the first place was because it was a fitting topic for the global economic crisis. Yes. There was an economic crisis. A crisis, for God's sake. My story was one that other people could probably relate to. Telling it would help them. With this in mind, I had the incentive I needed to write. Two thousand words later, I sent the draft to the director in Geneva before I lost my courage.

The day of my radio debut, I dressed up. It was a coming out party of sorts, and even though no one would see me, I wanted to look good. I had listened to recordings of David Sedaris. I had been coached over the phone by the host of "The Business," the show that my story would run on. I was as ready as one could be to tell the truth about who I had become.

A man greeted me at the studio in Zurich. Thanks to technology, I didn't have to go all the way to Geneva to record the segment.

"You're Chantal," he said, "I know you. I read your blog. I'm probably your biggest fan."

I didn't know I had fans so I didn't know what to say. Instead I smiled so big I must have resembled some kind of lunatic. Anyway, my fan's name was Mike and he was overseeing my session. He set me up in one of the studio's small recording rooms. I drank my water and reviewed my radio essays, silently enjoying the boost to my self-confidence that Mike had given me.

"So anyway, tell your story and if you fumble the words, say 'try again' and repeat the part you want," Mike said.

Try again. I could try again. I stood up to the mike. Yes, there were more chances than one to reinvent your life. This was the bigger story I was telling as I performed the one I had been hired to write.

What I Wish I'd Known
About *Mutter*hood

#21: No matter how much you want a baby, your wallet doesn't

I was your classic American cheapskate. I hoarded hotel bathroom minis. I saved paper napkins. And I wasn't ashamed to take twenty peppermints from every restaurant that was generous enough to put out a candy bowl. So imagine my distress when I ended up living in a country where restaurants charged for dinner rolls.

For me, the cost of living in Switzerland was the ultimate culture shock. I had moved from the US, where I collected pennies from sidewalks—no matter how dirty or wet—to Switzerland, a nation that was so rich, it didn't bother minting anything less than a five-cent coin. It was a penny-pincher's nightmare: I was living in a place where pennies failed to exist.

It took about five years, but eventually Switzerland worked its magic until even the best penny pincher in the world—a.k.a., *moi*— became price insensitive. In fact, I was integrating so well, I almost began to swear by Swiss Made at any price. Until, that is, I became pregnant.

When you become pregnant in a foreign country, it's as if you start your expat cycle all over again. Blame the hormones or blame your foreign country (much more fun), but the combination is lethal. Because even if, like me, you had begun to accept the extra charges for that bread roll even though your schnitzel wasn't exactly a bargain, your expatriate season of discontent will begin to grow all over again—along with your expanding midsection.

As an expectant mother with unexpected cravings, I could no longer ignore the cost of ice cream because its price per pint (more than twelve American dollars) could bankrupt me. If this thought hadn't chilled me as I reached for another Ben & Jerry's, the diaper section (21.95 Swiss francs for forty-two)—placed strategically near the checkout—did. Forget a heightened sense of smell or morning sickness; what made me sick during pregnancy was looking at the price of Pampers ($25). With one glance, these alone explained the low Swiss birth rate while also making the price of Chinese food look like a *Preishit* (the Swiss version of "a great deal," which comes complete with the word "shit" at the end, since the Swiss hate cheapness).

Having a baby was like most things in Switzerland, no matter how much you wanted it, your wallet didn't. But it wasn't only the prices. It was also the lack of selection. Take maternity clothes: there's only so long you can go around wearing long sweaters with your skinny jeans unzipped. At some point, you must concede that you need maternity clothes. This shouldn't be the end of the world: there are almost seven billion people on the planet, meaning there must also be millions of pregnant women walking around at any one time. Most of these people, I presume, prefer to wear clothes—a concept that seems earth-shattering in Switzerland: not because people are walking around naked, but because hardly any shops sell clothes for expectant mothers.

Where can you get maternity clothes in Switzerland? After some not-so-scientific research, my hormonal conclusion was: pretty much nowhere. Did the Manor in Baden—a huge (for Switzerland), five-story department store—have maternity clothes? No. Did the H&M in Zurich's Sihlcity shopping mall have them? No. Did Globus? No.

In the meantime, my pants were falling down along with my self-esteem, and I wanted to throw a tantrum (who am I kidding, I did throw some tantrums). The only place left to go—at least in Baden—was MoMas, a tiny maternity store with not-so-tiny prices, but it didn't care if my pants were falling down on a Tuesday—it only wanted my business on Saturday. During the week, it was only open on Wednesdays, Thursdays, and Fridays between 2 p.m. and 6 p.m. By the time I got off work, the store was closed and the only place that was open was a travel agency advertising shopping vacations in New York City.

Luckily, I had an equally frustrated pregnant friend who, around this time, had finally discovered the H&M next to Coop, on the Bahnhofstrasse in Zurich—even though its maternity section seemed like an afterthought, shoved in a corner of the basement. Here, you could choose from about five pairs of pants and five shirts. And at noon on a weekday, a bunch of pregnant career women, with little patience and time, were fighting over them.

Unfortunately, once I finally had enough clothes for my expanding stomach, my chest had to go and grow too. So once again, I spent many days in a state of discomfort, before my never-ending shopping mission led me to a nursing bra. The search finally ended at a baby store in Dättwil. For two bus rides, a mere 150 Swiss francs, and half my Saturday, I was the proud owner of a pair of less constricted breasts.

I also wanted to keep in shape during my pregnancy, so when my Speedo swimsuit failed to stretch any further, I searched the nation for a maternity version; after a few failed Saturdays, I turned to the Internet. It was easier, faster, and didn't involve my entire day. About ten days later, the Speedo maternity suit I ordered from a store in England arrived. After I waddled over to the post office to collect it, I found that the Swiss customs officials had charged me thirty-one Swiss francs in import duty. All for a suit that didn't even exist in Switzerland, not to mention barely cost twice that amount in the first place. But with the extra Swiss charges, came the extra American motivation to get my money's worth. So I paid Die Post an extra 50 percent for that suit and swim I did. Almost a mile every other day. Until the day before my daughter was born.

#22: Cheese is a homeopathic treatment. For your boobs.

It's a romantic idea: giving birth in a country known for its ski slopes, fondue, and storybook mountain girl. Oh, to have a Swiss-born, American baby. One who, unlike her "greater Chicago-land area" mother, will grow up naturally trilingual, international, and able to eat twenty-six pounds of chocolate a year without gaining weight. But let's be clear: I was never one of those people who dreamed of living abroad—let alone of having a baby there.

One thing led to another, however, and by age thirty-two, my biological clock began dinging and donging as much as the ten-story clock tower across the street (that is, every fifteen minutes, 24-7). My husband and I had been in Switzerland past our original expiration date, but we were enjoying our careers and the European lifestyle that accompanied them. This meant I would have to face my fear of childbirth in a country where I didn't yet know the word for morphine.

A year and two red lines on a little stick later, I began my education. I learned the German equivalents of "cesarean section," "epidural," and "please, no episiotomy." The very clock tower that had set off my own biological clock helped time my contractions as I lay on my sofa all night, wondering if this was real labor. It was, and I arrived at the hospital the next afternoon at nine and a half centimeters dilated—too late for pain medicine in any language, not that I could talk at that point anyway. So three hours later, there I was, the giddy survivor of natural childbirth. On my lap was the little baby I had been expecting. On my chest two days later was the large amount of curdled cheese that I had not.

As most mothers know, when your milk comes in after giving birth, the swelling can be excruciatingly painful. Since most women stay in Swiss hospitals at least four to five days after giving birth, there's plenty of time for the lactation consultants to administer Switzerland's natural solution to the discomfort: soft, cold cheese. Turns out I had known more vocabulary for pain medicine than I had given myself credit for.

Despite having lived in Switzerland for five years before giving birth, I had never eaten or cooked with quark, which has the consistency of ricotta, and is mainly used in desserts. But after wearing it, I didn't think I'd ever be able to taste something associated with a medical treatment, no matter how homeopathic.

Cheese, homeopathic treatments, xenophobia. Looking down at my cheese-covered chest, I couldn't help but wonder if slathering quark on a foreign mother's breasts was Switzerland's idea of a joke to those of us who were adding to the foreign population. (Unlike the United States, Switzerland does not grant citizenship based on place of birth.)

According to some Swiss midwives, though, a nice slice of chilled quark is the perfect remedy for engorged breasts and for pretty much any breast pain associated with breastfeeding. It's cheap, it's natural, and there are no side effects to the treatment, except for the mandatory shower one must take after the curdled cheese drips down your chest and into your belly button.

After confirming that I, the foreigner, was not alone in my cheesy treatments, I tried not to question them: when you live in another country, you accept that things are different. But when I mentioned that the dripping cheese was soiling my hospital bed, the midwife shrugged and brought me two Pampers—one for each boob—and placed them over the quark.

Not surprisingly, I decided not to have friends visit me in the hospital.

But the other people, well, I couldn't keep them away. The nurse, the cleaning lady, the cleaning lady trainee, the lunch lady bringing me a sausage salad I didn't order, somebody's lost husband. They all paraded in and out of my stinky room as I lay on my bed, center stage, wearing nothing but stretchy hospital underwear, cheese, and diapers. What had been a simple prescription for quark became a lesson in humility. An ice pack just wouldn't have been the same.

#23: Guilt is universal

Your friends warn you about the money-absorbing powers of diapers. Your cousin tells you about the sleepless nights. And your mother reminds you how it will all be worth it. But no one gets you ready for the never-ending trial, the one where you, the mom, are both the criminal and the jury. The one where no matter how you defend your choices, the verdict is "guilty."

My motherhood-induced trial began the day I found out I was pregnant. While the getting pregnant part was far from a mistake, it still marked the time practically every other choice I made possibly became one. I second-guessed what I ate, how I worked out, and why I was living in a Swiss canton that allowed smoking in restaurants. I couldn't even eat a hamburger without having a minor panic attack (I mean, what if the meat wasn't cooked all the way and I got toxoplasmosis!?).

I had no real reason to be paranoid. No real reason to feel guilty about taking a swim in Lake Zurich with my ever-expanding belly or walking past a smoker without holding my breath. I was healthy and my pregnancy was problem-free. Still, I bit my nails, picked my lip, and enjoyed a non-stop eye twitch. By the time I gave birth to Baby M, I had taken so many guilt trips I had practically acquired silver status.

And then came motherhood. It was time to go for the gold.

Like many new mothers, in order to convince the jury I was innocent, compromise became my middle name. If I couldn't do everything, then everything was what I would do. I would work 60 percent, be a mom 70 percent, and go completely out of my mind 110 percent. And I did it all while meanly thinking—as American society cheered me on from 5,000 miles away—that at least I wasn't *that* mom, the one who sacrificed everything in order to be sane.

My husband, since he was a father, seemed immune to guilt. He took three weeks of unpaid paternity leave and went right back to his old life, with the exception of Friday nights, when he babysat so I could go swimming.

"No," I told him. "You are not babysitting. You are watching your child."

"Right," he'd shrug, guilt-free, as he got out the PlayStation to play FIFA Soccer—his version of entertaining a baby.

While I swam, drowning in guilt for leaving Baby M for the insane length of two hours, I couldn't help but wonder why I was the one with all the remorse while my husband spent his limited father-daughter time redesigning his website. After all, it was guilt that kept me from eating cheese while pregnant. It was guilt that kept me pumping my breasts, even when my daughter would no longer nurse. And it was guilt—along with a little Swiss culture (for which I was grateful)—that kept me from going back to work full-time.

When people asked my plans (and they always ask a mother's plans), I'd tell them, yes, I was going back to work, but only on Mondays and Tuesdays plus one day working from home on Wednesdays so Baby M would only be in daycare two days a week even though I would be working three days a week. If it sounded like a mouthful, it was one; I was biting off more than I could chew.

My mother-in-law listened to my spiel, but didn't believe me.

"She'll take one look at that baby and forget about going back to work," she predicted, before Baby M was born.

Which probably would have been true, if I had been a child of the 1950s. But it was the twenty-first century and I had been blessed with something women didn't once have: choices. Thanks to Switzerland's attitude to professional part-time work, I had a lot of them, ranging from working 0 percent to 100 percent and everything else in between. But give an American woman too many choices, and she will take them all. When I thought about all that my weeks involved, I couldn't help but think my mother's life had been easier. As she tells it, when she went to college, her choices were pretty much: teaching or teaching. When she had a baby, her choices were pretty much: stay home or stay home. When I went to college, there were so many options that I double majored and still felt like I was missing out on something. Eleven years and a baby later, nothing had changed except my concentrations, which had now switched to motherhood and English copywriting in a world of Swiss German advertising.

"What are you going to do, sing jingles to your baby?" the older generation would ask. Then I would laugh a fake laugh and think about the alternatives: (1) a résumé gap or (2) a child raised exclusively by daycare workers born after 1990. Either way, the horror music played. Either way, the mental institution beckoned. Either way, I needed industrial-strength Advil. I was an American born in the 1970s. If I didn't chop myself in half, I wasn't whole.

When I dropped Baby M off at daycare for the first time, I waited for the jury. I was outside the daycare. My six-month-old was inside, immersed in a completely Swiss German world. My little pumpkin, for the first time in fifteen months, was not kicking me from the inside or the outside.

The sky was dark. Raindrops dripped down my black coat like tears. I waited for them to flow from my eyes as well. But instead, a strange thing happened. I smiled.

Stop the press. Hold the camera. Aim it at something you've never seen before like a selfish mother. Clearly, I was a good example of one. I should have been bawling, right? I should have been consumed with separation anxiety, no? But as much as I wanted to be Ms. Model Mom and get an "A" in motherhood, this moment would then involve feeling crushed, broken, and in need of a reality show with which to share my angst with the entire world. So that one morning, I failed. I didn't feel sad. I didn't feel guilty. All I thought, walking away from the charming little girl whom I loved, was, "well, this is kind of nice."

I should have rejoiced in that moment longer. Skipped to my desk in my new non-nursing bra, a binding device that was somehow, at that moment, the epitome of freedom. But as I boarded the train to go to the office, something terrible took over my mind, body, and soul. Ladies and gentlemen, there I was, Ms. Remorse-Free Me, sitting next to the window on my way back to 60 percent of my good old life as a professional working woman, watching my reflection as my smile turned to a grimace, all because I felt guilty for not feeling guilty.

#24: You cannot do anything right

Once you become a mother you realize something: no matter what you do, there will always be a stranger on the street who can't wait to help you do it better. This can make you crazy in Switzerland alone, but if you're an international mother like me and you drag your poor little thing to five countries in her first twelve months, then you will have more kinds of run-ins than even you had bargained for.

Switzerland: You should dress her more warmly. You should put socks on her feet. You should make sure the blanket doesn't ride up to her knees. You should get off the bus with the stroller facing forwards. You should not block the sidewalk with that stroller because another bus is coming in 11.53 seconds.

United States: She's crying. She probably has gas. What, you're just going to let her cry? But we have drops for that. This is America and we have something for everything. Do you have Baby Tylenol? That will solve her sleeping problems. Now, please sign on the dotted line before you place her in this high chair. We cannot take responsibility for injury, choking, or hot beverages that may or may not get spilled. No, I cannot possibly hold her while you sign on the dotted line. What if I abuse her by mistake or something?

Germany: *Entschuldigung*, are you something from our grocery store in that enormous stroller of yours stealing?

Ireland: Of course we have high chairs at this pub. Come right this way. Would she like to enjoy a Guinness coaster or does she prefer to suck on a Connemara whiskey one? Why did you bring baby food? We have Baby Mash. See, it's right here on the menu.

France: Ooh! A bébé! Kiss. Kiss. Voilà! One kiss for each fat cheek, bébé. Ooh, bon, let moi feed you the petit-déjeuner. Oh bébé, let moi wipe your runny nose. Oh bébé, mais non, can't you see dees toy worm eez better dan dees toy worm. The colors are so much more pleasing, on dees one n'est pas? Oh bébé, did moi hear you say "oui?" Très bien, bébé! Learn many languages, but only ever speak zem in French.

#25: See this blurry, prone-to-freeze image? That's your new granddaughter.

In 2006, I began my life in a country with a +41 area code in the most modern way possible: with a Chicago-based phone number. Throughout my seven-year Swiss career and counting, my friends and family have called me via landlines and cell phones as though I were across town, which has often made the 5,000 miles that separate us feel more like five.

"I love Skype," I used to think, if it's even possible to love a proprietary voice over IP service—or, for those of us less technically inclined—an Internet phone. But I loved Skype because it made my long-distance relationships easy, whether my relationships were ready to embrace its new technology or not. Some of them still struggle in a "what's-a-web-browser" kind of way. But most late adapters are now adapted, which makes a traditional phone seem something more appropriate for a museum exhibit than a conversation.

"I'm getting a new laptop with a built-in camera for Christmas," my overly wired mother bragged last year, stressing the words "built-in." She ended up getting a Kindle too. One technology leads to another, I guess.

During our progressing Skype years, thanks to both

training visits and webcams, my parents and I could finally hang out with each other live from our living rooms. 2-D was the new 3-D. And it was free. My entire family learned to love Skype. Skype had saved us from international disconnect and discontent. It was God of global living and it was great. Well, it was great except for the question my mother-in-law would ask every time my husband and I Skyped with her.

"When are you going to come home?"

The original answer was 2009, when my husband was on an expat contract with an expiration date. But since we were now on local Swiss contracts, our families struggled to accept that we were living in Switzerland indefinitely.

"When are you going to come home?" she would always ask again, when we didn't answer.

Then to avoid looking directly at her, we'd look around at where she was sitting: in my husband's childhood bedroom among old Pet Parade trophies and Tony the Tiger stuffed animals. And then we'd think, well, for an hour or two a week, we were kind-of, sort-of home.

For the first five years of my Skype career I was a satisfied customer. Sometimes thanks to the time difference, I could Skype the night away, going to bed with a raw throat but a warm heart. But my so-called love affair with Skype began changing as soon as my daughter was born. I suppose this was only natural because babies are born out of love and then they redefine it, changing your relationship with everything and everyone, including yourself.

Five days after her birth, Baby M was introduced to her grandparents for the first time over a Skype video. There, in front of a tiny webcam, her entire six-pound, twelve-ounce frame was transformed into a few billion oscillating electrons and beamed across the Atlantic and onto my parent's old Dell computer monitor. Never before had a blurry, prone-to-freeze image made my parents squeal with more delight. I was thrilled for them to meet Baby M. But it wasn't exactly how I pictured bringing my daughter into her grandparent's home for the first time. It was during that call that Baby M, together with a certain VOIP technology, began teaching me about love. Namely, that in order to love fully, one must engage in all five senses. You don't only want to admire a baby or sing to a baby. You want to hold a baby. Feel her smooth skin. Smell her freshly washed hair. Skype didn't make that possible. So the call was bittersweet, but bittersweet was the best we had. Wasn't that better than no sweet at all?

I started to have a lot of questions. Would we go home where ties to love and family were strong but the economy wasn't? Would we stay in Switzerland where my husband and I both had successful careers? What affect would modern technologies have on things like old-fashioned relationships?

When Baby M was thirteen months old, she began waving at a contestant on *Deal or No Deal* one day. Then she clapped and smiled at him. When he didn't respond to her, she was crestfallen and confused. How could it be? It was the same TV, the same screen where Grandma and Grandpa appeared when we Skype videoed them every week so they could watch her play. They waved to her. They clapped when she clapped. She reached towards them. They reached towards her. Yet this man, Jim, it said on his nametag, was oblivious to her existence.

Welcome to love and rejection, twenty-first century style, an era where it's never been easier to connect but never been harder to hug. Baby M didn't give up easily though. She touched the screen, trying to get Jim's attention. She thrived on audience participation and she did not consider anyone, even a man on a British game show brought via cable television to a Swiss apartment, excused from her performance. She clapped again. Waited again. Waved at Jim again. As I watched her react to his non-reaction, along with her inability to distinguish a grandparent from a game-show contestant, my insides pulled apart—even further apart than the 5,000 miles we were from home.

Home. When I was growing up in the 1980s, all of my extended family lived within a three-hour drive of Chicago. So did my husband's family. Throughout my first eighteen years, I saw my grandparents almost every Friday. We had something old-fashioned: a real live relationship. One that involved no planes, pixels, or media that hadn't been invented yet. One that involved a grandmother so connected to my life that she sat in the front row at all of my voice recitals; embarrassing me by practically conducting each of my solos from her place in the church pew. While Skype is great, it's not front row and center at a music recital. It can't embarrass you in front of your friends. Or come over when you don't invite it in. A real relationship, well, it can. And it does.

They say absence makes the heart grow fonder—but what happens when absence is replaced with presence, the virtual reality version? Many of my friends and I—both stateside and abroad—not only have Skype babies, but also Skype holidays. The Saturday before the real Thanksgiving holiday last year, I joined some of my expat friends in Zurich to celebrate. Throughout the gathering, various friends and families were Skyped into the living room via our host's fifty-five-inch Sony television, which like ours, is connected to a computer. As we ate turkey, various people joined our party. An old college friend in San Francisco. A set of grandparents in Chicago. An aunt from New York City. This was 2012, and this was the new normal. It even came with a new language—one where sound bites rushed back and forth between continents without much content connecting them. A language where Skype wasn't just a noun. It was a verb.

Since the birth of my daughter though, I've realized Skype is also something else. A crutch. Skype wasn't an option when my mother lived in Africa for two years in the 1960s. She's told me many times that she wanted to stay abroad but couldn't imagine not seeing her parents for such lengths of time. But would she have moved back from Gabon to suburban Chicago if she too could have beamed her parents into her living room once a week? Technology tricks us. It makes far seem close. Replaces absence with so-called presence. Pixels are powerful. Through them you can love, but not kiss. Talk but not embrace. Almost a year-and-a-half after Baby M's birth, we continue to Skype like it's a verb, but only time will tell what action it will have on this noun called modern love in the future tense.

Baby M is toddling now. Rarely does she want to sit still for a Skype video call with Grandma—if she even remembers who Grandma is since we only see each other "live" about twice a year. Despite my efforts to set my Skype stage with the proper props—Baby M's Fisher Price airplane, her soft toy ball, and her big bunny stuffed animal, she often walks off camera anyway, so Grandma gets snippets of action along with snippets of conversation, while I run to retrieve Baby M to return her to the only place Grandma can see her—in cyberspace.

Back within webcam view, I urge Baby M to clap with Grandma or laugh with Grandma, but instead she kisses her big bunny and puts her arms around its neck. Can I blame her? So I give Baby M a hug, adjust the webcam, and then Grandma puts out her arms and we attempt a big group hug. I close my eyes. The television and computer are radiating heat, so if I concentrate hard enough, I can almost imagine it is the warmth of my mother's embrace.

#26: The world's wonders are right in front of you

Before Baby M was born, Brian and I concentrated on one thing: seeing the world's wonders. We were expats. And we lived like it. Taking advantage of Switzerland's location in the heart of Europe, we traveled when and where the spirit (and great airfare deals) took us. Warsaw for the weekend? France on a Friday? Notting Hill next week? *Tak*, *on y va*, and sign us up. I printed out a map of the world and hung it on our fridge. After every trip, I colored in the countries I had visited.

Thirty-two years and thirty-two countries later, the possibility to add a little bundle of joy to my life was slowly announcing its expiration date. Didn't babies define happiness? I loved happiness. And even though I had plenty, I got greedy; I wanted more. When "joy" finally arrived, I took her home, jubilant. But it wasn't long before "joy" made me feel something else: sorrow. Instead of seeing the world, I was seeing spit up. I couldn't help it; I missed my old life.

Did I have a mental disorder? Everyone I knew was congratulating me, saying how wonderful a baby was and how I should enjoy every moment. But all I could do was smile and nod and silently wonder, which moment did they mean?

Was it the moment when I dripped from every orifice in my body (orifices that before giving birth I didn't even know existed)? Was it the moment at 3 a.m. when I was reminded I wasn't a woman, but a cow? Was it the moment when poop became the main topic of conversation at breakfast? (That is, if I even remembered to eat?)

The truth is, after Baby M arrived, my life as I had known it took a free fall. Warsaw on the weekend? I had taken less baggage to Warsaw than I did now to go across the street. Work out? Even if my husband was home, I felt like I had to ask his permission to leave the house. Go back to work? Great. I could feel guilty. Stay at home? Fantastic. I could feel like I had wasted my education.

The worst part was my dining room table. Where the silver candlestick holders had once been was a big, yellow electric breast pump slowly sucking the life out of me every time I looked at it—never mind when I used it.

Why was all of this surprising? Hadn't living abroad taught me not to expect instant adjustment to anything? Why would motherhood be any different? Despite what I had learned, I thought I would immediately fall in love with becoming a mom. Everyone said that was what happened. So why did I find myself silently regretting it?

Why did you want a baby? Stop. I wanted to stop asking

myself that. But since that thought usually happened at the same moment I was sleep deprived and spilling some preciously pumped breast milk, it only egged on other troubling questions, especially if I saw a reflection of myself in a mirror. I had bags under my eyes and an extra ten pounds around my hips. *My God, what did you do to your exciting expat life?* Stop. I didn't want to ask myself that either. Especially when my daughter finally began smiling. But my protests did no good. My thoughts babbled more than my baby. And since they were mean and selfish thoughts, I didn't share them with anyone. Instead, I let them ferment inside me like a Swiss Gruyère. For two years.

Then it snowed.

Of course, this particular snowfall was hardly Baby M's first, but at twenty-five months, it was the first snow she registered. We watched it from our window. "Snow!" she yelled, "Pretty!" She remained mesmerized for at least nine minutes, practically an eternity for a toddler. "Out," she said, "go!"

We prepared to go outside. That took approximately one decade. She wanted to wear her dirty diaper. She wanted to put her Migros rain pants on backwards. And she wanted to wear her sandals. I tried not to remember my old life, when I left the house exactly eight minutes before the train to the airport arrived, tantrum-free and perfectly dressed for the weather.

Practically a lifetime later, which included several bribes in the form of Gran Pavesi crackers, we were at the park. I took my daughter out of her stroller and set her in the snow. I was sweating from the effort it had taken to go two whole blocks from the apartment. *Do something,* I willed my daughter. *Do something to make all the effort in getting here worth it.* But she didn't do anything except stand there as frozen as an ice sculpture. Then, to remind me she wasn't a sculpture, she whined. And reached for me.

I sighed and held her for a few moments, debating whether we should go grocery shopping instead. But something—let's call it renewed patience—made me set her down in the snow again.

I began making little snowballs as she stood there. First I threw them. As her frown began to melt, I handed her little snowballs and she threw them. "More!" she said, until we had made so many snowballs that a patch of grass surrounded us.

"Walk," she said. She took a hesitant step. "Snow," she kept saying, as her pace quickened.

When we reached the park's fountain, that mercifully, was finally turned off, we made more snowballs and threw them into it. Each time a snowball self-destructed at the bottom of the fountain, my daughter shrieked with joy. "Snow!" she sang, her face registering total bliss, as if snow were the most amazing thing ever.

At that moment, I realized it was. Snow was amazing. It was white and cold and beautiful and I loved it. And that's when I realized how much I loved my daughter for making me remember that.

I felt nothing but peace and happiness. Thanks to my daughter, a new way of appreciating life had opened before my eyes like a flower. It was a world where small things were big and wonderful. It was a world where an airline ticket to an exotic country wasn't necessary to find wonder. Instead, wonder was right in front of me, waiting to be discovered. It was in the form of my little girl in an oversized pink coat and pink boots. She was going to make sure I didn't miss a minute of it.

"Walk! Snow," she said.

Inspired by her words, I began to sing a song I had sung as a child, with a newfound sense of awe floating along with the melody.

My daughter smiled. "Mommy. Snow," she said. She couldn't have summed up the moment better—even with a verb. We threw another snowball in celebration of her thirty-five-year-old mother's ability to finally see snow as clearly as a two-year-old. I held her close, my lips warm on her cold cheek.

Then she decided to take off her gloves and my newfound love of motherhood took a commercial break.

"Aren't you going to put your gloves back on?" I asked.

"No!" she said.

I shrugged, feigning indifference and made her another snowball, which she took with her bare hands.

"Oh," she said, "cold!" She dropped the snowball like a hot potato and looked at me with the most wonderful expression: as if she had just watched a horror film.

"Snow is cold. That's why Mommy wants you to wear your gloves," I said.

"Oh," she said. Then she cocked her head and looked up at me like I maybe, actually, might have had a few words of wisdom to offer.

Now there was something to love in a daughter. So as she held out her hands for me to re-mitten, I was smitten. Her tiny appreciation for my common sense was yet another reason, two years after becoming a mother, that I finally loved my new and wonder-filled life.

What I Wish I'd Known
About Being A Foreigner

#27: You can increase your cheese tolerance

As an American, my cheese world used to consist of Kraft macaroni and cheese, Velveeta, Cheez Whiz, and if I was going gourmet, fondue in a box. And then there was Easy Cheese. The Spam of the cheese world, Easy Cheese came in a can and my grandfather loved it. After a holiday meal at his home in Chicago, he'd get out the Easy Cheese along with some crackers, and we'd squeeze out our cheese in swirly lines, like other people squeezed out toothpaste.

My cheese world was pretty much processed to perfection, but then I moved to Switzerland. All of a sudden, I was living in the land of cheese and I didn't know what to do because there wasn't any Velveeta. There wasn't any mac and cheese. And there wasn't any Easy Cheese.

I had entered a world of Swiss cheese, which was not without pain. First, there was my introduction to Raclette, an easily meltable Valasian cheese made from the fresh milk of cows that have grazed on alpine pastures. Easily recognizable by its strong smell, Raclette is melted and served over potatoes or bread and is a popular festival food. So naturally, the first time I experienced it, I was in a newly constructed tunnel since the Swiss celebrate completed construction projects like Americans celebrate capitalism. It was easy to find the Raclette stand, since all smells led to it. And while the Raclette tasted great despite its overpowering odors, which the tunnel emphasized like a microphone, the brass bands serenading my meal should have celebrated elsewhere—or handed out earplugs.

My next foray into the Swiss cheese world was via a beverage. For months, my husband had asked me, "Have you tried it yet?"

Of course, until I drank it, he would not reveal its ingredients and I had to admit, it wasn't bad; it tasted like soda. But then I found out the truth.

"Rivella is made from what?" I exclaimed.

Whey. Whoa. Whey? I wasn't even sure what that was.

Then I toured the cheese factory in Gruyères and found out that whey is what drips off cheese and should rightfully be put in the garbage. If cheese deems whey not worthy, why should I? But the Swiss crafted a popular drink from nothing other than cheese excrement, so I have to give them credit—this is a country that loves its cheese.

Regula, our neighbor, was no exception to this love. To thank my husband for teaching her how to use text messaging on her newfangled cell phone, she invited us over for Raclette. Brian protested, but dinner was not optional.

Later, I asked Brian, "What's the big deal?"

"Do you know how much cheese she eats?" he asked me, having already endured one Regula Raclette while I had been away.

When we entered her apartment, sitting on a tray near the dining room table were at least thirty slices of Raclette, ready for us to individually melt on her tabletop grill. It was a ten to one cheese ratio. But I already knew my Raclette limit. And it was three slices.

On my fourth slice, which wasn't optional in Regula's company, I tried to lessen the impact by only eating the cheese with half its usual potato and pickle accompaniments. After that, I retired my cheese tray on top of the Raclette grill, but Regula immediately put another slice of cheese on it.

"Nein. Danke."

"You can't be full," she said, looking at the pile of cheese sitting on the serving plate. "I usually eat at least ten slices."

"But you're Swiss," I said.

"You'll have another," she said.

As my next slice melted on the grill, my stomach bubbled along with it, a strange duet. I wanted to tell Regula that I had grown up in a world where cheese came in cans and that my stomach was still getting used to the real stuff, but she wouldn't understand. The only thing the Swiss sold in cans was vegetables and fruits. So as I scraped the melted Raclette from the grill pan and onto my plate, I took a deep breath and tried to pretend I wasn't eating it.

After the fifth slice, I hid my grill pan on the other side of the potato bowl, where Regula couldn't reach it. She saw what I had done though, and went to the kitchen and pulled out a bag filled with at least twenty more slices of Raclette.

"What will I do with the rest of this good, fresh cheese?" she asked.

I shrugged. I felt bad but my stomach felt worse. Regula shook her head at her ungrateful guest and continued to eat slice after slice of cheese.

A few months after that dinner, I was finally seeing progress when it came to my new cheese world. I could eat fondue one night and Raclette the next, all while enjoying an Emmentaler sandwich for lunch. I was proud of my new cheese tolerance and so when my grandfather celebrated my Chicago visit over Christmas by opening a can of Easy Cheese, I figured, piece of cake.

Although I enjoyed making the shape of a Swiss flag with the Easy Cheese, I could barely eat the result. The cheese was a texture and taste I had almost forgotten and it took all the willpower I could muster not to spit it out. Closing my eyes, I grabbed my soda to cover the taste of the Easy Cheese as fast as I could. This wasn't real cheese. It never had been.

"Good, huh?" said my grandpa, squeezing out some more Easy Cheese onto his cracker until it was piled so high it resembled the Matterhorn.

"Yeah," I said, trying to smile.

"Here, have another," he said, setting a cracker onto my plate.

I stared at it, that plain cracker, and it was a sad thing. Because Grandpa was passing me the Easy Cheese. And that cracker? I was going to leave it naked.

#28: You are the scariest thing in Switzerland

Someone fears you? It's a shocking discovery for a skinny white woman. The first time it happened to me, I was teaching an advertising copywriting class to undergrads at Virginia Commonwealth University when one of my students trembled as he presented his headlines to me during the second week of class. I was impressed—not with his work, but with a power to be feared I never knew I possessed. This feeling was novel and cool—but also short-lived. That is, until I moved to Switzerland and realized the scariest thing to people there was a foreigner and I was going to be staying a while.

My neighbor feared foreigners so much she installed a special alarm on her apartment door in addition to its double locks. The alarm was louder than an ambulance when it went off, and since technology was not Regula's strong point, it went off practically any time she opened the door. Or maybe, as a foreigner one wall away, I inspired it.

In any case, after installing the alarm, Regula also began locking herself in the laundry room while she washed sheets. You never knew when one of Baden's knife-wielding foreigners would hide out in our third sub-basement and attack, she said. To her it didn't matter that the building automatically locked at eight and that the motion-sensored lights in the hallways made it impossible to hide undetected. Don't go down there after nine, she lectured. But I never listened. What did I have to fear? I was the feared.

While Regula was having nightmares about people like me, I was having dreams about her. These dreams involved taking her high-pressure washer and using it against her paranoia with the same determination she used against my balcony's moss. Because when she locked the laundry room door to shut out the foreign criminals, she also shut out the empty-laundry-basket types who wanted nothing to do with crime and everything to do with dry towels. My key was rendered useless when hers was left in the keyhole on the other side of the door, so I always ended up having to beg for entry.

"It's me," I would call as I knocked.

Then the door would crack open as Regula peered out.

"Sorry," she'd say, flinging the door wide open while repeating her usual line about trash, danger, and foreigners. "I don't mean you," she'd add. She never did.

There are very few places in the world as shiny and safe as Switzerland, and yet if you talked to my neighbor, you'd think she lived in the Motor City. I have never, in eight years, seen anyone in the basement other than her, my husband,

and the spiky-haired teenage coiffeurs from the first-floor salon with whom we share the laundry room. While I find these teenagers scary, it is only because at the age of sixteen, they are already out of school and spending most of their time smoking on my front steps. However, my neighbor is scared of Switzerland in an "I'm going to be attacked and killed" kind of way.

To be fair, she was once mugged at umbrella-point by the Limmat River.

But actually, there are bigger things to fear in Switzerland than umbrella carriers—the main one being the Swiss People's Party (SVP). This ultra-conservative political party has exaggerated danger and criminalized foreigners in their political advertising and policies to such an extent that almost every foreigner I know in Switzerland feels unwelcome. This is unfortunate for many reasons, since according to the 2013 International Migration Outlook, migrants have a positive impact on Switzerland's economic development. In fact, Switzerland and Luxembourg are the countries whose tax coffers are most boosted by foreigners. Nevertheless, most SVP ads, which are always prominently displayed in public areas in Switzerland, make it clear that anyone who isn't white or Christian is not only unwanted in the land of cheese and chocolate, but also dangerous to

Swiss people and the Swiss way of life. During the minaret controversy in 2009, when an SVP initiative to ban the construction of the minarets was put to vote, one of their ads showed a Muslim woman wearing an abaya and a niqab standing next to a drawing of minarets piercing the Swiss flag like missiles. The ads were so offensive that even human rights organizations protested. But by then it was too late; the images were in almost every Swiss train station—and imprinted in every Swiss resident's mind.

While I don't necessarily agree with recent votes that limit immigration and ban minarets, I do find it refreshing that any citizen in Switzerland has the power to change things should they collect 100,000 signatures within eighteen months. But with this power, should come some responsibility for the way initiatives are communicated. When political messages result in a frightened population that reacts to scare tactics, something is wrong with the system. Because while foreigners like me see Switzerland as beautiful, safe, and clean, thanks to the SVP, some Swiss no longer do. When I witness my neighbor living in fear in a country so pristine that the scariest thing is someone like me, I can't help but shake my head. Because when I fly over Zurich in an airplane and look down, I see nothing but tiny houses and manicured rolling hills. It's the only country I know of where the perfection seen from 15,000 feet holds true up-close. Zurich has a skyline composed of church steeples, a wide pedestrian street with shops selling thousand-franc coats and three hundred-franc shoes, and a population that appears to be able to buy everything they need—with the exception of a sunny day.

To me, Regula's fears seem a bit ridiculous, but then again I'm a foreigner and Switzerland itself seems a bit ridiculous. The country is so well taken care of that things often look fake. Trashcans double as mirrors, benches are such a bright red you wonder if the paint is dry, and everyone competes for a non-existent gardening award. No one ever arrives late for anything. They speak four different languages yet understand one another. You can ride the bus for years (and eat your lunch off the shiny, clean floor) without someone actually checking to see if you bought a ticket. And companies send you a bill for anything from detergent to dryers—after they've already delivered your goods.

Which naturally brings me back to the laundry room.

As I cleaned out my lint, I felt something creepy. Regula's eyes; they were on me. Suddenly self-conscious, I paused, wallowing in fear from something even more trivial than a foreigner—dryer lint.

"I'm going to wait for you, so we can go upstairs together,"

Regula said.

"Oh, okay," I said, disappointed that I would have to finish my lint retrieval under her strict supervision.

Finally I set down the paintbrush, thinking the dryer couldn't get any cleaner. But then Regula grabbed the brush and proved to me otherwise. As she removed lint from crevices of the dryer I still didn't know existed, I thought: she was right. Switzerland was scary. In fact, it was probably the scariest place I had ever lived.

#29: You will never be Swiss

The Swiss don't organize things; they engineer them. Timetables. Trash. Trees. Everything has its place and nothing is out of place, except (in my very paranoid American opinion), the people at the pool.

My local twenty-seven-yard swimming pool has only one lap lane, set in the center of the pool. It is labeled, for "sport swimmers." But if this pool were to live up to my version of its Swiss potential, it would be divided into six lanes: each organized according to swimming speed. But instead, the pool is usually chaotic, as if the *Schwimmbad* were another country. It's filled with adults attempting to swim laps, while kids jump off diving boards inches from their faces and others paddle diagonally or toss beach balls across the pool, as if the space were theirs alone.

To me the place seems like an invitation for a lawsuit, but that's because I grew up in a country run by lawyers instead of people. Since the Swiss run their own country, they have a very different approach to "danger" than most English speakers. It's called personal responsibility. And it's much more practical and less expensive than a lawsuit. For example, in Switzerland, if there is a big hole in the street, it's your responsibility not to fall into it. If your coffee is hot and you drink it, that's your problem. And you shouldn't hide knives or open flames from children. Instead, you should give toddlers the necessary tools to carve a large radish and then have them carry it in a parade complete with a burning candle inside of it.

While I didn't like the idea of my toddler carrying a candle in a parade (luckily she was only interested in doing so for about thirty seconds), I did like the Swiss concept of personal responsibility. It was ten times better than the concept of "blame someone else for my stupidity" that most Americans subscribed to—at least if they could afford a lawyer. But unfortunately, culture kind of sticks to people like melted Raclette cheese sticks to a pan. So even when I tried to scrape off my American paranoia at places like the Swiss swimming pool, it was difficult. Back in Chicago, our pool had strict swimming rules; if you ran around the pool in my hometown, the lifeguard would whistle at you and you'd be scolded. You couldn't use a gigantic floating device wherever and whenever you pleased: only between 9 a.m. and 11 a.m. on Saturdays. And diving into the pool was not allowed, even if no one else was swimming.

But 5,000 miles from my hometown in the United States, going to the pool feels more like going to the circus. Without lanes and lifeguards—it's a free-for-all, seemingly made all the more ironic by the country in which it takes place. And if you're a serious swimmer, but aren't quite at the Olympic level necessary to keep up in the pool's only lap lane, you've got to go claim your spot in the water and fight to maintain it. And somehow, the paddlers who don't want to get their hair wet can't wait to get in your way.

The first few years I was in Switzerland—due to something Americans call politeness and the Swiss call passivity—I never accomplished anything: I couldn't seem to get cheese from a cheese counter, get a seat on a tram, or swim like a normal person at the pool. The Swiss asserted themselves and I, feeling claustrophobic from my lack of American personal space—not to mention my fear of a potential lawsuit if I touched someone—backed off.

It took a couple years, but slowly I learned to assert myself even though I always felt paranoid about doing it. I'd barge into the line at the ski lift; I'd claim I was next at the meat counter, and I'd push ahead of others to get a seat on the bus. I felt about as natural as a *Cervelat* doing so, but my new strategies served me well. Soon I decided it was also time to use them at the pool.

At about the last 200 yards of my one-mile swim, a woman started paddling in my little space. I tried to avoid hitting her, but if she noticed there was another swimmer about three inches from her face, she didn't show it. So the next time we were headed for a collision, I decided not to worry about a little body contact. Not surprisingly, we crashed. I excused myself in the usual Swiss way, "Oh, Entschuldigung."

Normally, at this point, I would have moved, but this was the new "Swiss" me, so I resumed swimming and she resumed paddling: neither one of us prepared to worry about hitting the other. As I approached her again, the American in me began to surface, so I altered my stroke to prevent another run-in. I avoided her, but in changing my stroke to do so, I accidentally splashed her. I was about to say "Entschuldigung," again, but I didn't have the chance. Because she splashed me, using her hands like a little kid. Then she said something in Swiss German. All I knew was that it certainly wasn't "Entschuldigung." Nevertheless, I kept swimming. Except now, every time I passed her she splashed me and yelled something. What had I done wrong? I didn't know.

Shaken, I jumped out of the pool and ran for the shower. Then I rushed to get dressed and get the heck out of the Schwimmbad and back to the civilized Swiss world.

I was drying my hair in the common area when my splasher, now also clothed, came and stood right in my face.

"You're a foreigner, aren't you?" she said.

Before I could think of an answer and translate it to German, a man walked into the common dressing room.

"Do you know what this foreigner did?" she asked him.

The man looked at us, confused. I couldn't blame him. We were in a country known for peacekeeping and she was speaking in voice that suggested otherwise. I tried to defend myself with my Deutsch and my hairdryer, but it did not go well. The man, whose face pleaded neutrality, shook his head and disappeared into the men's dressing room while I wished I could disappear through the floor.

"You do not me know," I said: a pathetic comeback, but all that my language skills and mindset allowed. The truth? I didn't know who I was at that moment either. I thought I had been acting Swiss, but she had labeled me a foreigner.

I didn't appreciate being singled out as a foreigner, but as time passed, I began to think that maybe, in a way, this woman had been right. I was an American who had been trying to act Swiss. I had been an impostor; someone who couldn't ever understand what it meant to be Swiss. Someone who would never be Swiss, no matter how hard she tried.

The reality was, I didn't enjoy acting like someone I wasn't—even if sometimes it did get me a seat on a crowded train. So now, when someone gets in my way at the pool or cuts in front of me at the cheese counter, I embrace my upbringing and let them. I end up waiting a lot longer for cheese than I should, but at this point, I'm okay with that.

#30: You will not change Switzerland, but Switzerland will change you

After living in Switzerland for six years, I sometimes had grand illusions that I was becoming Swiss. In my finer moments, I was spitting out genaus, playing the national card game Jass, and listening to my American husband practice his alphorn in our living room. In these moments, I thought, "I can't go home again."

At that point, despite the way my big American smile had been tamed by years of Swiss indifference, I remained optimistic—I loved my lifestyle here and I thought becoming Swiss was still a possibility. Not necessarily in the way of passports or permits, but more in the way of acceptance. Can you blame me? I came from a country called "The Melting Pot." In the United States, almost every family has once been foreign. But the longer I lived in Switzerland, the more I began to understand its foreigner statistics—both emotionally (especially when I realized that my Swiss-born, Swiss German-speaking daughter would always be one) and intellectually.

Switzerland defines a foreigner differently than my country. In Switzerland, once a foreigner, almost always a foreigner. This is why 23 percent of Switzerland's population is "foreign,"—and why Switzerland has the highest percentage of foreigners in Europe behind Luxembourg and Lichtenstein. In many other countries, most of Switzerland's so-called foreigners would be natives. Instead, people who are born in Switzerland and never leave and give birth to their children here, two, three generations, people who know nothing of the country whose passport they hold and everything of the one they don't: these are Switzerland's foreigners.

If there's a consolation prize for foreigners in Switzerland, I've won it. I mean, to most Swiss, I am the "good" kind of foreigner. You know, the white, native English-speaking, high-earning kind of foreigner. But even as a "good" foreigner, living in the land of chocolate is bittersweet. You can love it—the public transport, the quality of life, and the beautiful lakes and mountains. But when it doesn't love you back, you find yourself between an Alpine cliff and a hard place. Suddenly you realize forty-eight peaks over 13,000 feet surround you and that acceptance in such a place can be more than an uphill battle. It can be an insurmountable one.

Speaking of battles, in a confederation that claims to be neutral, here's where they happen: underground. There's a reason most Swiss laundry rooms used to be bomb shelters.

If you'll recall, my first time in the bomb shelter/ laundry room was the hardest. If you'll remember, the multilingual discussion was something about how to leave the dryer door open at a forty-five-degree angle, how to clean a soap dispenser that wasn't dirty, and how use a paint brush to remove any trace of the worst pollution known to Switzerland: lint.

Fast-forward a few years though, and as you've read, things were going well in my Swiss bomb shelter. I had come a long way since 2006 with my Swiss neighbor. After a year, I knew her first name and had graduated to "du" status. After two, we were eating dinner together with a German-English dictionary on the table. After five, we had dessert together on Christmas Day, *ohne* dictionary.

And then none of this mattered.

Because she found a coin in our washing machine.

I opened my door not so long ago to find my neighbor, only I barely recognized her.

"You..." she said. Her hands shook in anger and she could barely talk in complete sentences. She wagged her finger and pointed a five-franc coin at me like a gun. Her temples throbbed and her voice wobbled.

"How could you do this? Thanks to you, the washer is broken and I can't wash my towels! And I need to wash them. I need to wash them right now! You are disrespectful and irresponsible. You make a mess of everything!"

Holding my half-dressed daughter, I blinked at this ball of anger waving money at me. Who was this? This wasn't the woman who had taught me how to make a proper fondue. This wasn't the woman who had offered to take me to the hospital when I was in labor. This wasn't the woman who had driven me to a farmer's field so we could pick flowers together. This was a woman who was Swiss, yelling at a woman who was foreign. Because at that moment, even after six years of dinners, gossip, and gambling lessons at Grand Casino Baden, that was who I was to my neighbor.

"Take it," she said, pressing the heated coin into my palm.

I hesitated. Coins don't have names on them. How could she be so sure it was mine?

"Take it, you! And never do something so horrible as this again!"

My hand closed around the coin, and in doing so, I subconsciously submitted to the prevailing "I am Swiss and therefore perfect" attitude—or at least at that moment, I gave up trying to fight it. Who was I to say the Swiss weren't perfect? Every time I opened a newspaper, my own country self-destructed right before my eyes. In contrast, Switzerland didn't have a word for "wear and tear" or a tolerance for mineral buildup. So a Swiss would never, heaven forbid, leave a coin in a pocket before starting a load of clothes—

even if besides dirty laundry they also had a colicky baby and a headache. It isn't in their DNA.

After the coin incident, my grand illusions of becoming Swiss became just that: illusions. Seven years after moving to Switzerland, I may have changed, but nothing else had. I had seen it in my neighbor's eyes the day she gave me the coin from the washer. I would always be The Foreigner. More than I would ever be her friend.

Despite the clash of attitudes that have occurred between us, Regula and I continue to eat Raclette together and share the occasional glass of wine. I try to make amends and do things as close to her hopelessly high standards as humanly possible for a mere American mortal. I do this not because I'm passive (although not speaking a language very well can make you naturally that way) but because I'm the one living in her country and not vice versa. There will always be things about Switzerland that I question, but that's because my culture is always along for the ride—even when the train is 100 percent Swiss.

At the same time, there are many things that Switzerland has taught me about myself (namely, how painfully American I am) and about what my own country could be doing better (especially when it comes to public transportation and work-life balance). But I've also learned that life as an outsider is challenging. It seems like every time Switzerland begins to feel like home, something happens that makes me realize it never can be. Maybe these feelings about an adopted country are universal to foreigners everywhere—I will never know. But the harsh, straight, and orderly line that exists between citizens and foreigners in Switzerland—at least in my experience—tells me that despite the alphorn in my living room and the Swiss German coming out of daughter's mouth, Switzerland will never, truly, be home—no matter how much I love living here. That's why I sometimes find myself wearing white socks and sneakers, listening to American public radio, and dreaming of owning my own home again in the United States. After all, these days more than ever, America is a country of imperfections. It's a place where someone who leaves a coin in a pocket before starting a load of laundry just might fit in again.

About The Internet

Google Search not necessary.
Here are some resources on Swiss and expatriate life
(in order of shameless self-promotion, of course):

One Big Yodel
onebigyodel.com
A blog about what happens when an American (*moi*) lives in the heart of Europe

Writer Abroad
writerabroad.com
Surviving (and thriving) as an international creative person

Swiss Life Book
swisslifebook.com
Life in Switzerland. The not-made-for-TV version.

Zurich Writers Workshop
zurichwritersworkshop.com
Providing inspiration and quality instruction to passionate, active writers in Zurich

Geneva Writers' Group
genevawritersgroup.org
Bringing together over 200 English-language writers from twenty-five countries

World Radio Switzerland
worldradio.ch
The only English-language radio station in Switzerland

Swiss News
swissnews.ch
The international magazine of Switzerland

Swiss Info
swissinfo.ch
News about Switzerland, business, culture, and more

Hello Switzerland
helloswitzerland.ch
A magazine written by expats for expats living in Switzerland

My Girlfriend Guide to Zurich
mygirlfriendguide.com
Tips about news and happenings in Zurich by women, for women

Diccon Bewes
dicconbewes.com
Writer, traveler, chocolate lover, and author of *Swiss Watching*

Newly Swissed
newlyswissed.com
The latest trends in Swiss culture, design, oddities, and tourism, as well as tips on how to settle in Switzerland

Frontier Magazine
fmagazine.ch
English-language magazine for the Lake Geneva area

Expatica
expatica.com
News and information for the international community

Expat Women
expatwomen.com
Inspiring your success abroad

About Books
What I'm glad I read about Swiss and expatriate life

Beyond Chocolate: Understanding Swiss Culture
By Margaret Oertig-Davidson
Contrary to popular belief, there is more to life in Switzerland than chocolate and this book helps outsiders understand how Switzerland and its people tick.

A Moveable Marriage: Relocate Your Relationship without Breaking It
By Robin Pascoe
Are you a trailing spouse or about to become one? Here's a book on how you and your marriage can survive your first–or tenth–international move.

Swiss Watching: Inside the Land of Milk and Money
By Diccon Bewes
Want to go beyond the Swiss stereotypes and deep into Switzerland to find out what Swissness means? Then this book is for you.

Expat: Women's True Tales of Life Abroad
By Christina Henry de Tessan
No matter where we choose to live abroad, this anthology demonstrates that some things about expat life are universal.

The Xenophobe's Guide to the Swiss
By Paul Bilton
The blurb says it all. This book is definitely "A frank and funny look at what makes the Swiss Swiss."

La Place de la Concorde Suisse
By John McPhee
The army in Switzerland can seem mysterious, but not if you read this journalistic study of its role in Swiss society.

GenXPat: The Young Professional's Guide to Making a Successful Life Abroad
By Margaret Malewski
How can you thrive when working in another country? This book has many answers.

Cultural Intelligence: A Guide to Working with People from Other Cultures
By Brooks Peterson
If you get a job in Switzerland, this book is a great introduction to any diverse workplace.

Inside Outlandish: Essays about Feeling at Home (in Switzerland)
By Susan Tuttle
Enjoyed *Swiss Life: 30 Things I Wish I'd Known*? Then you would probably also like this collection of essays about life in Switzerland as an outsider looking in.

Living in Zurich Guide
By The American Women's Club of Zurich
This book bills itself as "The Most Comprehensive Guidebook To Life In Zurich As An Expat" and it's hard to argue with that. Like everything else in Switzerland, it's quite expensive, but if you're new to Zurich, it's worth every franc.

About the Author

Originally from Chicago, Chantal Panozzo arrived in Switzerland in 2006, relieved to discover a country where people can actually pronounce her name. Her essays have appeared everywhere from *The Christian Science Monitor* to *Swiss News,* where she wrote the monthly "Expat Adventure" column for three years. She has also served as a *National Geographic Glimpse* correspondent, been commissioned to write and perform a corporate drama by *World Radio Switzerland*, and her essays have appeared in several best-selling anthologies. In 2010, she co-founded the Zurich Writers Workshop. A recipient of the Rosalie Fleming Memorial Humor Prize, Chantal divides her time between copywriting, writing, and blogging (*One Big Yodel* and *Writer Abroad*). She is currently at work on a novel, and would like to remind everyone that really, it's okay to live in canton Aargau. www.chantalpanozzo.com

Acknowledgments

Danke to my husband, Brian. Without him, there would be no Swiss life. Since the greatest gift a writer can be given is a chance to live outside their home country, I have him to thank for our wonderful eight years abroad.

Merci to my Switzerland-born daughter, Baby M, who will always understand Swiss German 110 percent more than I do. You have provided an endless new array of writing inspiration and a lot of love.

Grazie to my grandparents, Oliver and Marion Nielsen, themselves huge supporters of anything artistic, who left me just enough money to finance my dream of writing a book. And of course, to my parents Donald and Susan Nielsen Panozzo, for always supporting what I wanted to do with my life and telling me to do it—even when it took me thousands of miles away from them.

Grascha fich to Anneliese Herzog Poulakos, who introduced me to Kelly Jarosz and Emily Lacika, with whom I co-founded the Zurich Writers Workshop in 2010 and finally discovered the English-language writing support I needed while living in a German-speaking country.

Thank you to these friends, writers, editors, translators, and authors, who have provided encouragement, contacts, and critiques: Kelly Jarosz, Emily Lacika, Kati Clinton Robson, Susan Jane Gilman, Janet Skeslien Charles (who recommended Lizzie Harwood, the editor of this book—thanks to Lizzie, for making this book as good as it could be), Philip Graham, Jill Prewett, Tom Kees, Jean-Marc Vanot, Bill Harby, Dianne Dicks, Elizabeth Smith, Julie Sensat Waldren, and Coz Cotzias at the VCU Brandcenter (who swore at me to write more in my life than advertisements).

Say Hello. Or Grüezi.

Chantal talks about life in Switzerland on her blog, One Big Yodel. She would love it if you dropped by to say hello in whatever your official language of choice may be. You can also come by her website www.chantalpanozzo.com or follow her on Twitter (Writer Abroad), or send her an e-mail: chantal@chantalpanozzo.com.

If you want to get an automatic e-mail when Chantal's next book is released, you can sign up for her mailing list at www.swisslifebook.com. Your e-mail address will never be shared and you can unsubscribe at any time.

Word-of-mouth is crucial for any author to succeed. If you enjoyed this book, please consider leaving a review on your online bookseller website of choice or on Goodreads, even if it's just a line or two. It would make all the difference and is very much appreciated. *Merci vielmal.*

CPSIA information can be obtained at www.ICGtesting.com
Printed in the USA
BVOW02s0026271015

424014BV00002B/5/P

encore at the opera house.

"Isn't this fun?" he whispered to me.

I faked a laugh and gulped down the rest of the champagne. Electronic music blasted and more dancers came on the stage. Rolf, Natalia, and Anja swayed to the beat. Or maybe it was my head spinning.

"You never know, maybe I'll be discovered!" Edi said. I shrugged, not wanting to burst his bubble. But the only other audience member besides us was definitely more interested in his personal lap dance than what was happening onstage. And from the looks of him, he probably wasn't interested in men who sang Frank Sinatra at strip clubs. But who was I to judge?

"Woo hoo!" Anja yelled, as some new girls stripped. She waved her cigarette in the air. Ashes fell onto the table like confetti. I sat back to avoid getting burned. Rolf ordered another round of champagne. Natalia got up to prepare for her next song. From the stage, she winked at Rolf. Rolf waved. He took a photo of the girls on stage with his iPhone. Edi got out his iPhone too. But instead of snapping one of the girls, he wanted me to take his photo standing in front of the stage now that he was a performing star.

I took a photo of Edi and then I sat down and took a deep breath, which resulted in a coughing fit. *I'm going to leave now*, I thought. As I stood up, my purse dropped to the floor. I reached down to pick it up and a few of my business cards fell out.

"Where are you going?" Edi said.

I stared at my business cards.

"To the bathroom," I said.

*

At 2 a.m. I stood on my balcony. *Hello, Disney World.* A medieval clock tower, a castle, and a cathedral surrounded me. Even after living in Switzerland for two and a half years, I was still in awe, because they were real, they had been here for centuries. I leaned against the railing and considered something else that was real: my feelings. The much-sought-after job I had once thought would be the answer to my problems of identity and acceptance was creating as many issues in my life as it was solving.

I climbed into bed when the clock tower dinged three times, and Brian snuggled next to me, the blinking red light on his BlackBerry illuminating the room. I pulled away from him and gazed at the pulsing pink ceiling.